I0797764

HAUNTED
SOUTHWEST
FLORIDA

CHRISTOPHER BALZANO

Published by Haunted America
A division of The History Press
An imprint of Arcadia Publishing
Charleston, SC
www.historypress.com

All images courtesy of the author unless otherwise noted.

First published 2025

Manufactured in the United States

ISBN 9781467159494

Library of Congress Control Number: 2025937576

Notice: The information in this book is true and complete to the best of our knowledge. It is offered without guarantee on the part of the author or The History Press. The author and The History Press disclaim all liability in connection with the use of this book.

This book is dedicated to two very different women who made it all possible.

The first is Gina Taylor. Her love of history and confidence in my abilities helped at every step of the process. It also helped that she allowed me to steal her research on the city of Fort Myers.

The second is Deanna Mulhern, my true muse throughout so much of this book. She has been the inspiration for many of my legend trips and my companion on more than one. More than anyone's, it was her voice echoing through my head with her mantra, "Honor the story." I hope I have done that here and made her proud.

CONTENTS

ACKNOWLEDGEMENTS

Unlike the stories in many of the books I have written, many of these stories have been in my back pocket for a few years now. I want to start out by thanking every person who told me their legends, on and off the record. I'm hoping I've given your moments the respect and honor they are due. My kids, Ella and Devin, have gone from tolerating my talk of ghosts to coming with me on many of my adventures. Thank you for your patience and encouragement. I have been to almost all of the locations mentioned in the book, so I need to take time to thank those who have tripped with me on them, including Natalie Crist, Deana Mulhern, Richie Ferrara, Lee Ehrlich, Joshua Edilla and Stephanie Nordin. A special thanks to all the librarians who have allowed me talk at your libraries and get information from your patrons. I would not have been able to write this book without the backing and knowledge of Gina Taylor of True Tours. A special thanks to Gemma Rose for her energy and research and Nicole Upton for her help getting me through my last two books. A special shout-out to Tiffany Thamer-Phelan and Phelan Paranormal Group.

I would like to thank the many writers and researchers who laid the groundwork for many of the stories in the book: David Hoes, Kimberly Rebman, Dr. Brandy Stark, Mark Muncy, Evie Alexander, Carol Mahlor, Kim Cool and Laurie Champion.

I would also like take a moment to show gratitude to the online researchers and posters who helped me in my research. I have tried to include all of you in my bibliography, but so many of the old notes I had led to links that were dead. If you see your ideas in my words, please reach out.

INTRODUCTION

I'm going to have to apologize up front. I was born and raised in New England. I am not from Florida and have spent only sixteen years here, which some may think qualifies me to write this book and for others will be an excellent reason to pass off anything that I might have to say. I understand, being as protective of some of the places I wrote about in the early days of my career. I got the same pushback when I wrote *Haunted Ocala National Forest*, and I live four hours away from that. I can tell you that I have been researching the paranormal here for the last eight years, traveling from town to town to capture people's experiences and track the ghostly legends they tell. I know the history of some of these towns better than the people who live there, but I do not think that makes me qualified as an expert. I am sure there are some who will read this book and tell me I got this detail wrong or that they've never heard that story and they've lived there their whole lives. I get that.

I call my podcast *Tripping on Legends* due to this fact. This title has always had a second meaning for me. I often find myself tripping over the history of places. In other words, I get it wrong and love to be corrected. I deal with folklore and storytelling. The work of a historian is just something I dip my toe into when I need to understand a legend's context and use it to connect to other ghostly motifs. I can tell you I have left some historical details about these stories out, not to make the story fit my narrative better but so that the details don't weigh the story down without adding anything to it. A great example would be the story of McGregor Boulevard in Fort Myers.

Charlotte Harbor, one of the many landscapes in haunted Southwest Florida.

The whole saga of Maurice Pearl, Tootie McGregor, the Smithsonian, the number of bodies that were discovered and the historical dead bodies that could account for the bones is so complicated, ever-changing and overgrown that it would take away from the story to get into its complexities.

I am more amazed about this part of the story: True Tours in Fort Myers has been walking through downtown for more than a decade, and its stories are told from a script, which guides then accent with their own voice. The original script was lost, but photocopies were made and then photocopies of the photocopies were made and then the company decided to rewrite it. While I do not subscribe to this number completely, in that script, the official body count was 103. I've seen that number several times and have gotten into debates about it. When True Tours wrote the new version, someone mistook a 3 for an 8, and new guides began saying 108. This number was repeated and made it all the way to Internet chats and Reddit posts until the number shifted to 108 in most retellings. There are times when the history is not nearly as interesting as the crooked paths folklore takes.

I have been to nearly all the locations in this book, although not always as a legend trip. That means the stories here are the kind that draw me in, and this book is not a compendium of every ghost story from the area. I am not drawn to haunted hotels or spooky restaurants for my podcast, so I do not cover them here. There are plenty of those to visit, and they can be found in other books. I recommend many of them. I work on a theme that drives how I design my books, which stories to include and how I approach telling them. As I started to look at the mythology of this area, I began to feel more and more that there was something at work in many of the stories, like a cloud wafting over the coast from time to time to obscure the beaches and beauty with an echo of something darker, refusing to be silenced by the passing of time. Those stories made it into this book.

Some tales I still have not unlocked, and I do not tell stories I haven't unlocked yet. Those are the ones I sweat over when I speak at libraries and tell and retell to friends, trying to get it right. The true crime story and hauntings of Smallwood come to mind. One of my favorite ghost stories is of Lilian Place in Daytona, but when I wrote about that area, I had not totally wrapped my head around it, and it was left out. Smallwood is the same way. Telling a ghost story so tied to the living is tough if you trip over the details. I felt the same way about the Braden Castle and Center Place and the Fisherwoman of Lake Arcola in Avon Park. They sit there, taunting me to solve them enough to jot them down, as if documenting a ghostly legend is as easy as a jot. Someday. Maybe.

The biggest issue locals have with this book may be how I define Southwest Florida. There are no standard lines drawn, no consensus about what that actually means, and as I started to thumb through my stories to see which would fit in, the existing definitions of "Southwest Florida" failed me. Many would say it's the Gulf Coast from Bradenton or so to Naples and Everglade City—but how far inland? Route 41, also known as the Tamiami Highway or Tamiami Trail, felt like a natural border, with towns a little to the east. The issue for me was that went all the way to Miami. That's a totally different world than Sarasota or Fort Myers and is so well covered I would be walking in someone else's footprints. It was hard not to write about the Labor Day Hurricane and its impact on Islamorada, a story so vast it may deserve its own book someday.

The Sidney Berne Davis Art Center of Fort Myers, the other side of haunted Southwest Florida.

Ultimately, it was two roads that set the boundaries for me. The first is Highway 75, and while I travel north of Tampa and St. Petersburg, stretching almost into Central Florida, it felt right. It fit my theme. The second is what I call Spooky 17. If you've driven that road during the day, you've been annoyed at the constant speed limit changes and a bit confused about the contrast that happens between miles. You'll be driving over farmland, as flat as any in Florida, and then be at a stoplight in front of a historic district in Bowling Green or Bartow a moment later. If you've driven it at night, you know the other feeling. You want to roll up your windows, not because of a smell or for fear of someone trying to jump into your car but because the darkness seems to want to get to you. You feel more likely to see a black-eyed kid in your backseat than be the victim of a crime. The trees lean into the road when you arrive at the small towns, like they're trying to pull you in.

That's the undefined feeling I let guide my hand when choosing stories. When I move over the pavement of these places, these highways become filled with landmarks of legends. Miles go by, and I think of which story I know in the next town and how it chills me. For me, 75 and 17 are like mystic numbers, so most of the stories I legend tripped by taking these made it into the book—proper borders be damned.

I honestly hope that works for you if you have already purchased this book. If not, keep an open mind, believe in curses and feel free to get in touch with me to tell me the stories I left out and the ones I got wrong. I love when I'm told I tripped on a legend.

CHAPTER 1

A CONQUISTADOR, A CURSE AND THE NAME GAME

Of the many legends told at the Silver Springs Park, the oddest might involve true love, an elephant and a curse placed on a horrible man. According to the story, Hernando de Soto was in the process of conquering the western side of Florida when his beautiful bride arrived on the continent. He wanted everything to be perfect for her and for the Natives to see how beautiful she was. All this was proof of his divine providence. He decided to show her off with full attendants riding majestic elephants. They made their way through the thick swamp toward what is now Silver Springs and came across a particularly clear area where the water looked as if it touched heaven itself. Being a god and understanding things like clearing bodies of water, de Soto declared the water shallow and safe and stepped aside. He waved to his wife's entourage to go first so everyone could see them and awaited the applause from the other side. It never came. Instead, all plunged into the water, killing Mrs. de Soto, all her attendants and the elephants they rode upon. It was in that moment, sure that the tribe he had looked to impress had ambushed them, that he decided to lift any pretense of niceties toward them. To this day, in that part of the park, you can still hear her screams and the drowning of the animals. On some nights, you can still find her glistening white ghost trying to cross the water and crying when she can't.

If you know anything about history, you know almost none of that legend could be true. Not only did Hernando de Soto not really love his wife, but also her last name was not de Soto and she did not die in Florida. She became governor of Cuba and held the position even after her husband died.

Sunset at the armament at Fort De Soto where dead soldiers are seen.

That legend is the kind of narrative our main villain inspires. Throughout history books and tales of ghosts, there is one Spaniard whose name comes up time and again. It seems an odd thing for so many rumors to be born around a man who contributed so much to Florida's history. On the other hand, speculation about his cruelty and conquering has inspired fear and misunderstanding. An embellishment here and there makes sense. The official diaries and records of his journey across Florida were lost by his secretary, Rodrigo Ranjel, for hundreds of years, enough time for stories to take hold. Of course, even that part of the story is exaggerated.

The most far-fetched piece of gossip about Hernando de Soto may also be the part of his history that makes the most sense. De Soto had a vile curse placed on him, and the state of Florida is still feeling its effects today. It is okay if you do not believe in curses. They flower on faith, so you can just call it a series of coincidences all swimming around one man. Hernando de Soto was a plague on early Florida and stirred the imaginations of those caught in the echo of his trip to the state.

De Soto was born sometime around 1497 in Spain. By the time he was in his early twenties, he had already been to the Americas and assisted in the conquest of Nicaragua and the taking of Peru. He had a reputation for being vicious but also cunning. While the Inca ruler Atahualpa was in captivity, he took a liking to the man. He told de Soto secrets of the empire that would lead to its easy conquest, all while de Soto was ransoming the ruler for all the gold and silver his followers could deliver. Before de Soto was forty, the Spanish king had made him governor of Cuba and granted him the right and the mission to seize all Florida. He took his job seriously. In 1539, he landed in Southwest Florida with over six hundred men, two hundred horses and the understanding that all that was in front of him belonged to Spain and was rightfully his for the taking.

While most of the conquistadors made their name through their ruthlessness, de Soto was a different breed. Take this legend about a beautiful Native American princess he encountered in South Carolina named Cofachiqui. He seduced the young woman and convinced her and her tribe to take his men in, all the while stalking her mother through the woods in an attempt to kill her and planning to massacre her people after they discovered where the rumored gold was in that area. That was pretty much how he handled the people he discovered in Florida. His men ravaged their way north through the state, killing, spreading disease and doing whatever they wanted to the women they found along the way. All the while, de Soto led with his silver tongue, convincing communities to make deals with him and earning enough trust that tribes would give him their best trackers to help locate the treasure he sought and the next victims he would strip.

All this was enough to earn him the bad vibes of those he abused, but the official curse came when he turned west. In modern-day Live Oak, not too far from Tallahassee, de Soto came upon the village of Napituca on the Suwannee River. He immediately tried to convince the Timucua he found there that he was a god, a ruse that had worked on so many other tribes he had come across. They were not buying it. His reputation had marched ahead of him, including the kidnapping and murder of one of their chiefs, named Aguacaleycuen. The Timucua pretended to welcome him in but secretly planned to murder him and his men under a flag of truce. De Soto got wind of it through some interpreters. He was ready. While his men pretended to be casually scouting the area and in no position to fight, he agreed to the meeting. What ensued became known as the Battle of the Ponds. When the Timucua attacked, the Spanish were ready and immediately began counterattacking with their full army and cavalry, killing most of the tribe on that first day. Two hundred survived and retreated with their remaining chiefs. De Soto and his men waited them out rather than charge onto the soft, swampy ground. The next day, convinced they were facing defeat, the Timucua surrendered, knowing they could not trust the evil men they were giving themselves over to. The Spanish did not disappoint. All the men, including the chiefs, were executed. The last Timucua, speaking for those dying around him, placed a curse on de Soto and all those who bore his name.

In that area of Florida, the jinx seemed to take form. While the Spanish continued to move west, the troubles of settlers continued long after they were gone. Spanish missions established in the area were constantly hit by storms and mysterious fires. Development took years. After the War of 1812, when Florida officially became a state, officials tried to put the state capital there, but the men sent out to scout the area inexplicably got lost and were never able to find the town. The bloodiest conflict of the Civil War, the Battle of Olustee, in which three thousand men were killed, took place in that area. Whispers of the curse circulated when many of these same places started to experience ghostly activity.

Even in death, Hernando de Soto offered a creepy story. Historians credit him with being the man who found the Mississippi River, and the people there saw him as a god. When he succumbed to fever in May 1542, his men did not want to damage that reputation. It is said they weighed him down and sank him in the Mississippi. Although several locations are said to be his grave, no one knows exactly where his body is. His ghost is seen at all those memorials, looking lost and confused.

HERNANDO COUNTY

The real impact of the curse is mostly felt in Central and Southwest Florida. Places that bear de Soto's name or where he is known to have spent time tend to be more haunted. Take Hernando County: the people there named it in de Soto's honor but then changed it to Benton County as a thank-you to the man who helped pass the Armed Occupation Act of 1842. Finding that they did not agree with his ideas on slavery, they changed it again, to Hernando. Stuck between the haunted Ocala National Forest and the creepy, lore-filled Green Swamp area, Hernando County may be one of the most haunted areas of Florida, the jewel of which is Brooksville. In addition to several haunted hanging trees, Spring Hill Cemetery has been a favorite place of people looking to spook themselves. The cemetery, which was established as a burial location for African Americans in the area, was rumored to be used, mockingly, by locals to lynch them. Ghosts of men swinging from the tree at the center of the cemetery have been reported at night. There are also stories of wispy figures seen there during the day and people feeling the sensation of being pushed out. Cars sometimes have handprints on them when they leave, as if someone has tried to force the entire car down the road.

Whenever you look at lists of the most haunted places in Florida, Brooksville's May-Stringer House is likely to be featured. John May bought the land after the Armed Occupation Act and built the house in 1861. As tragedy and death befell the family again and again, whispers began of a curse. People staying there say they can hear what sounds like children walking across the floor, and one of John's children, Jessie, appears to kids and talks to them. There is also a man in uniform who hangs out on the second floor. Over the years, people working there or coming in for repairs have quickly left and refused to come back. Today, the owners run successful ghost tours and overnight investigations there. The paranormal is big business in Hernando County, and they embrace their ghost stories.

The curse does not end there. Originally, Fort De Soto was built in Brooksville. The fort failed and had to be taken down when the fort's original

Iron Bridge, on the edge of Hernando County, an area named after de Soto.

troops realized it had built it on phosphorus deposits and could not get well water in. Then there is the Withlacoochee River, which separates Hernando County from Sumter County. It is considered the deadliest body of water in Florida with the numbers of the dead boosted by older folktales and legends told by the tribes who originally lived there. Everyone in the area knows not to swim in it, especially the area near Iron Bridge Crossing. It is hard to find someone who does not know someone who died in the water, and reports of unusual deaths go back as far as 1896. The people who came before de Soto said it was peaceful, but after he left, they experienced what Floridians would tell campfire stories about hundreds of years later. There was even one death chalked up to injuries sustained when a man was impaled by a mastodon bone found in the riverbed. Maybe that explains the story of de Soto's elephants.

The Singing River

Other places were named after the Spaniard. He was seen for years as a true founder of the state. Old Desoto County broke off from Manatee County in 1887 but was broken up into smaller counties in 1921. That means the curse extends to not only Manatee but also modern-day Hardee, Charlotte, Highlands and Glades, all of which have a deep tradition of weirdness.

There is a ghostly love story told in Bradenton, the seat of Manatee County, that is as much a part of the personality of the city as anything in its history. When the moon is just right on the Manatee River, you'll see the two canoes coming from either shore. Both have dark figures inside, yet somehow, the light from the moon and the stars illuminates them. Then music starts. Beginning with a low hum, it rises, sounding more and more like human voices singing. It crescendos as the two boats meet each other. Then both disappear, the music hanging on its final note like a coda before abruptly stopping. A few moments later, the sounds of traffic and river life continue as if the lovers were never there.

And maybe they never were.

The legend gained popularity years ago and is even immortalized on a series of plaques close to the spring that set everything in motion. She was the daughter of the Calusa chief, and he was the son of the Timucua one. The two tribes hated each other, and the only thing separating them was the Manatee. On the river, they could talk to each other and even conduct

Left: A boat ramp from the Singing Manatee River.

Opposite: A depiction of the haunting at the Manatee River. *Used with permission.*

business. One day, the two youths saw each other on the water and began to talk. Soon, as happens with the young, they fell in love. Knowing neither side would approve, the two would canoe out to each other by the moon and meet in the middle. Soon, that was not enough. The man proposed to his beauty, saying they could run away with each other to someplace where no one cared where they came from. She told him she couldn't.

"On my side of the river there is a spring my people drink from. Once you have tasted that water, and I drink from it often, you can never be without it for too long or it will drive you insane. I can't move away from the spring. Without it, I can't survive."

Being young, the man said they would make the most of it and maybe even sneak across the river to drink when the urge became too great. She loved him too much to say no. As they kissed, they became overwhelmed with singing coming from all around them. He was so scared he wanted to jump into the river to escape, but she calmed him. It was the sound of her ancestors, she said. They were blessing their marriage. "How can that be?" he asked.

"Long ago, a different tribe was across the water. They were violent and angry and threatened to kill every Calusa near the river if we did not surrender to them. We were not fighters and knew we could not defend ourselves. The oldest and wisest of the tribe went out to meet the invaders. They lined up one by one on the shore and began to sing the song of our people. Then, staring at the people approaching by boat, they walked into the water holding hands, the music still coming from their mouths until they drowned. The other tribe was so scared by this show of will that they sailed back across the river and left the area. Now they sing whenever something monumental is about to happen so we know to keep one eye on them and one eye on the future."

He could see the ghosts of these people standing on the surface of the water as she spoke. The music got louder. That night, they sailed back to his side. They were surprised when his family took her in and rejoiced at the union. After a short time, she began yearning for the waters of the spring and became obsessed with returning home. Her husband voiced his opposition, knowing if he went with her, he would be killed, and if she went alone, she would never return. She pleaded until he agreed to risk death for her happiness. Oddly, they were welcomed to the Calusa side with fanfare and cheering. The chief saw the same thing in the young man his daughter had seen and welcomed him with open arms. The young man ended up becoming chief of the Calusa and unifying the two tribes in that area, and they lived happily ever after.

The other version of the story is not so nice, but it explains why a large ghost ship is also seen emerging from the water on full moons. It was passed down by Egmont Key Lighthouse keeper and constant contributor to local folklore Captain Charles Moore. Pascual Miquel, also known as the Butcher, was obsessed with a commodore in the Panhandle who sought to catch and kill him. The Butcher would take a small boat onshore and follow the man, who did not know what he looked like. That eventually led Miquel to the commodore's daughter, whom he fell madly in love with. In the dead of night, he kidnapped her and sent her down to the Manatee River, where he had been hiding most of his hauls. The young lady, named Carlota or Charlotta, was not a willing girlfriend, but the Butcher was so in love he would do anything to please her. Knowing she was a great lover of music, he strung harp strings from the windows of the cabin where she was being held prisoner and across every porthole on the ship. "Every time the winds blow," he promised her, "you will hear beautiful music." The first time he took off to conduct another pirate adventure, she escaped from the cabin and found herself in the middle of a river she could not swim across. A storm started to hit the area. Knowing she might never be rescued, she made her way to the hull of the ship and began making holes in it. Then she found where the munitions were kept and set them on fire. As the boat sank and the men jumped ship and the storm raged, she stood on the deck, singing to the music being made by the wind until it sank.

DAUGHTER OF THE DEVIL

A similar love story plays itself out only a few miles away from the Singing River with an even closer connection to de Soto, this one involving his daughter, Sara. No one is quite sure where the name Sarasota comes from. People have offered their own theories over the years, but there is no direct translation in any known language. In 1906, George Chapline, a fairly new resident and the son of the local judge, told his version in a story titled "The Legend of Sara de Soto." People fully embraced it, causing the history of the area to shift based on a ghost story.

According to Chapline, when de Soto arrived in Florida, he was not alone. His beautiful daughter, Sara, traveled with him along the coastline as he devastated the tribes he came into contact with. She was a much gentler soul and took pity on those her father looked to rule. When they reached modern-day Sarasota, her empathy reached its peak. A young Seminole named Chichi-Okobee saw her one day as her father's entourage passed by and immediately fell in love. He allowed himself to be caught by de Soto's troops in the hopes that she would see him and feel the same way. His odd plan worked. She returned his affections, but he soon became sick with a deadly fever. For several days in the prison camp, she cared for her new boyfriend, and he made a miraculous recovery. Unfortunately, she came down with the same sickness. Chichi begged de Soto to allow him to nurse her using the techniques of his people, even bringing in a famous healer from the Everglades named Ahti. All efforts failed, and Sara de Soto died.

Chichi again fell before the brutal conquistador, asking that Sara be buried in the nearby bay, where her soul would be safe for eternity. Hernando gave in. Chichi arranged a burial in the water and led three boats out among the tides. The first carried Sara's body, decked out like the Seminole dead would traditionally be; the second had Hernando and a few dozen soldiers faithful to Chichi; and the last held the grieving boyfriend and more of his men. When they got to the middle of what is now Sarasota Bay, Chichi asked all his men to get into his boat, overloading it. He then set Sara's on fire and requested Hernando leave by himself. As the smoke rose higher and de Soto sailed back to shore, Chichi commanded his men to hack at the boat they were sailing in. All of them drowned, but their souls remained behind to protect Sara for all eternity.

Sara, Chichi and all his soldiers remain in the bay to this day. It is said that when whiteheads appear in the waves, it is the soldiers scaring evil spirits away from the young lovers. They also protect Sarasota itself. Their active spirits are the reason the area rarely gets hit by hurricanes when other towns around it do. You can even hear the singing of the men on clear nights, with one female voice rising above the others.

It does not take a historian to know that almost none of this story makes sense. De Soto was not the kind of man who would give in to the requests of his captives. He would never have gotten into a boat full of his enemies with machetes. All that aside, the story fails on some basic levels. De Soto, who died at the age of forty-two, never had a daughter. Moreover, the Seminole tribe did not exist until several hundred years after his death. Then there is the fact that Chapline clearly said he was writing a story to celebrate the city he loved, not documenting historical fact.

Truth rarely gets in the way of a good story, though, and Sarasotans fully welcomed his fictional history. In 1916, they held their first festival in Sara's honor; locals Genevieve Higel and J.B. Chaplin played the parts of the star-crossed lovers. The weeklong celebration was a huge hit. It continued yearly until 1957, when the local Jaycees changed it to a Scottish theme to mark the shifting demographics of the city.

None of that changes the haunted feeling of Sarasota Bay, which has a disproportionate number of haunted locations around it. A man dressed all in black walks Coquina Beach, and people are known to hear voices whispering and singing. Some think this may be de Soto himself, dressed for the funeral and waiting for his daughter to return. The music is heard less than twenty miles from the Singing Manatee story—less if you sail a boat. The Gator Club, built in 1912, is said to be haunted by its former owner, Mrs. Worth, and the spirit of a former madam from back in its brothel days. There might be several mischievous children around as well, pulling pranks on patrons and staff. The Green family, murdered in 1887 by the patriarch of the family, still walks Rosemary Cemetery, pushing people who approach their graves and walking around other parts of the cemetery like they are its caretakers.

And then there is Mary. She may be the most famous ghost in all Florida, the subject of countless YouTube videos and dozens of segments in documentaries on ghosts. She walks the rooms of Keating Hall on the campus of the Ringling College of Art and Design, interacting with the students. Rumors say she was a local prostitute brought in to satisfy the rich clientele of the Haven Hotel, the original name of the building. She fell in love with one of her clients and maybe even got pregnant by him, and he killed her to stop the scandal. Others say she took her own life by hanging herself in the third-floor stairway when the man rejected her, accounting for why so many over the years have seen her ghost hanging there, sometimes crying.

All the different accounts may be due to the different states of mind Mary may be in. Some wake up to her hovering over them, not much more than a skeleton in a tattered dress. There is a feeling of anger and dread. This is Mary on a bad day. It might be the version of her reaching back from her unknown grave. Others see her in the corner of the room or as a reflection in the mirror, wearing a beautiful long dress with her hair done up, almost as if she is admiring their life. Smiling Mary might be remembering a good day. This version is most frequently glimpsed when people are getting ready for the day or freshening up before a big date.

There may, instead, be more than one Mary in the building, and they may not all be named Mary. Over the years, students have seen her only in quick flashes and describe her differently. Maybe some are echoes and impressions left over from flashes dating back to the 1930s, when the building was a hotel. While the legend initially feels like a tale told time and again in ghost stories, there may be some truth to part of it. When investigator Paul Benstine looked into the haunting years ago, he found something that shifted the backstory while explaining how it may have gotten started. His group, Paranormal Extreme, interviewed historical societies and combed through records. They also were allowed to investigate the dorm, where they got the name Minnie Belle Hughes on tape in the stairway. They discovered a woman by that name who had died in the hotel. While described as an "undresser" on the official death certificate, she was a prostitute who worked out of the hotel. She was also African American. Digging deeper, they learned her body had been rushed out of the building to prevent the press from knowing what had happened, and an autopsy was never conducted, which is odd, considering that the cause of death was determined to be kidney cancer. There is no way to determine that without an autopsy, and doctors at the time, if there had been one, would not have been able to be that specific. Adding to the weird, the notes about the cause of death are written in ballpoint pen—which were not in wide circulation at the time and which does not match the pen used on other parts of the death certificate. The undertaker who signed it died years before he supposedly filled it in.

These are just the kind of things that happen in the shadow of de Soto's legacy.

The Witch of Arbuckle Creek

The town of Lorida in Highlands County is pretty much a ghost town now. Most think the witch had something to do with it. In the early 1940s, a man desperate for love contracted the local "herbalist" for a love potion. She agreed to make it for him and asked to meet on the bridge by the light of the next full moon. He waited and waited until the night arrived and made his way to the bridge with all the money he had. She took one look and laughed. She was changing the price. Now she wanted his firstborn son. The two got into an argument, and he accidently pushed her off the bridge, impaling her on a banyan tree.

The man weighed down the body and left the area, love potion in hand. It took only a few days for the herbalist's body to rise to the surface. She was a respected person in the town—everyone had used the herbalist at one time or another—but they could not bury her in their Christian graveyard. Instead, they buried her under an oak tree near the bridge. Within a week, the old woman began to appear on the bridge. Sometimes she would suddenly be there, standing in the middle of the road, and cars would almost go off the road trying to avoid her. Other times she perched on the bridge itself, glowing white and pointing a finger at passing cars. In town, the effects of the curse were felt as well. Businesses started to fail, and people left town.

The citizens dug the herbalist up and buried her in the next town over. That did not work. She continued to perch and stand, and businesses continued to fold. More and more people were leaving. They dug her up again, this time burning the body and her shack in the woods and scattering the ashes in nearby DeSoto County. It was too late. The town went under (this is an exaggeration, but not too far off). Even that did not stop the witch.

She still appears on the bridge, especially on full moon nights. It's a dark ride through the back roads to get there, especially as you travel dark miles past business and restaurants and into the center of the town. She points and she perches. She has even been known to get into people's cars and is seen without warning in rearview mirrors.

There are other spirits at the bridge, perhaps trapped by two curses. A little boy is seen playing underneath it who laughs and disappears. He has been known to pull the lines of people fishing off the bridge before diving into the water without a splash. He never comes back up. The little boy also likes to play with boaters. There is a loading ramp right there, and when people back up their trucks to place their vessels in the water, they will suddenly be released and float away. Then the laughing is heard. Every so often, people also hear a man yell at the ghost, as if all he needs is a little discipline. Maybe the witch did get the man and his firstborn son.

Bloody Bucket

Travel down Route 17 and you'll hit your share of haunted legends. Once you get past Arcadia, the next place to look for is Wauchula. Located in Hardee County, it has one of the most misunderstood but active hauntings on the west side of Florida. You'll get different versions of the story, but most of the details come down to three things: go to the Bloody Bucket Bridge by the light of the full moon. Fill a bucket with water and watch as it turns to blood. Then listen carefully, and you'll hear the sound of babies crying and splashes in the water when no one is there.

The most popular version of the story comes from folklorist Charlie Carlson in his book *Weird Florida*. It is the story of Ludmilla Clark, a former slave who came to the town after the Civil War to become a midwife. Through the trauma of a lifetime of giving up her own children and seeing the way the world was going, she began to think the world needed fewer people in it. She intentionally killed some of the children she was delivering. She would bury them down by the bridge over the Peace River, the same place she dumped the afterbirth. When she began to kill more frequently, the townspeople realized what she was doing and banished her. Still, she went to that bridge with her husband some nights, dumping empty buckets she claimed were full of blood and crying. Eventually, she took her own life at the spot.

Most locals know the story is completely made up. A fiction writer wanted to explain why the road and bridge were called Bloody Bucket, so she made up a tale for Halloween that got passed along until it became truth. The real reason for the branding was a bar that used to be at the end of the road. It was so wild that the people cleaning up at night would have to mop up teeth and blood. They would then dump their buckets of blood onto the road.

The fiction was able to gain popularity because the bridge really is haunted. Visitors on full moon nights might not see the water in their buckets turn into blood, but they can hear babies crying. The sound comes from all around when you are standing on the dock. You can also hear the splash of water next to you, close enough to see what is causing it. But the water is undisturbed. There is nothing there.

FORT DE SOTO

And then there is the military base in Tampa Bay named for the man himself. It might be the best example of a place where the curse knocks things off balance.

The soft thump, unheard unless you are listening closely and the sound of the waves against the beach is not too loud, may be what gives her away. It's the sound of a hard rubber ball bouncing against the wall. His mom slipped it to one of the nurses, who gave it to him. Mom and son didn't work it out ahead of time. She just knew, when she walked the grounds and put her hand up against the wall and heard it, that her son was alive and playing with the only toy he had. It was their signal.

He died of yellow fever; people say that for sure. It's never mentioned whether the mother also died at the fort. She had other little ones to take care of and was sheltering in one of the other buildings reserved for those quarantined but not overly sick. She held each of those children tight, but when they fell asleep, she strolled around the other buildings until she came to the hospital on the edge of the water. He would not be in the lowest level. Even then, that was where they kept the morgue. On May 9, 1980, the nearby Skyway Bridge would fall after a storm caused a passing ship to run into it. On that day, people discovered in the water would be stored in that same basement morgue, but that was a lifetime away.

The mother put her hand to the wall as if she could feel her boy's heartbeat. It did not stop after he died. She would walk the night, not fully understanding why she was not even allowed to see his body. She put her hand on the wall. She heard the thump against the wall.

Fort De Soto has not been a quarantine hospital for almost one hundred years, and the little boy must have died well before it closed. That does not stop his mom. Most nights she can still be seen, a glimmering shadow glimpsed and disappearing before being seen again. She fades in and out, but her crying does not. It echoes steady but sorrowful and continues all through the night. She is walking around searching for her boy. It would make sense that she is exploring other places. Then you hear that knock against a wall that is no longer there, and she is walking toward the sound and toward you. She does not seem to notice you as she gets closer. You'll hear the thump of a rubber ball before you see her approach, put her hand on the wall and cry harder.

No matter how many stories are told and urban legends created about the haunting, seeing or hearing her is not proof that she exists. Instead, it is the

The view from the remains of the old hospital at Fort De Soto.

sadness that carpets the remains of those buildings. It comes on as suddenly as the stars when the sun sets on Fort De Soto. You never see them coming; you just notice something has changed before you realize it is all around you.

Fort De Soto plays out the curse perfectly. The original intent of the base was to reinforce the one already established at Egmont Key, basically making it an afterthought. It never fired its guns at an actual enemy. Shortly after the first troops arrived, it gained a reputation for being hot and miserable and swarming with bugs. Soldiers were sent there as punishment for things they did wrong at other garrisons. No one wanted to be there. The number of enlisted men dwindled until defending its walls was a formality and not a mission. It became a nature preserve and then a quarantine hospital for people coming into Tampa Bay.

Through all this, it has been haunted. While it was still an active base, a soldier could be seen coming out of the water and collapsing on the beach before disappearing. No one could ever name the soldier; no one had ever died there in battle. He still comes ashore at dusk. A fisherman notorious in the area for his womanizing walks the shoreline on the way into the fort. He flirts and then vanishes. He was not even killed in the county, but this is where his soul returns. Then there are the constant conversations overheard in the barracks. People with recording devices pick up fragments of people talking to each other even though they are alone in the room. There you can also see people looking over your shoulder in the glass on the displays. Turn and they are gone. Nighttime at the worn foundations of the barracks means cries from people who are not there. Daytime there means maybe seeing one of the ghosts of the many victims of suicide at the Skyway Bridge jump, their bodies fading before they hit the water.

And the woman at the hospital, looking for her son, bouncing a ball trying to make contact: you hear her cry even when you can't see her.

You do not need to believe in curses for them to be real.

CHAPTER 2

WHO PLAYS AT THE OPERA HOUSE?

Agnes probably does not sit in the corner anymore, at least not when there are people in the room. She considers all of the Heard Opera House in Arcadia, often referred to as the Arcadia Opera House or just the Opera House, her personal playground.

She loves to explore the second floor of the building, especially when new people come in. The visitors catch her out of the corner of their eye playing on the old projector now displayed in the hallway, and people onstage spot her in the back during performances: just a little girl with plain long hair, most times wearing a simple white dress. She may be spotted in the orbs flittering around, balls of light seen with the human eye and not a trick of bad photography. That is a rarity, though. Usually she is felt: just a sense you are not alone and an odd lightness in the air. More than that, even, she is heard. She runs up and down the steep stairs leading to the theater, skipping almost as if she is playing hopscotch without a care about whether she falls. She laughs as she runs through the halls and giggles as she watches the people come in and out.

She is most well known for the little tricks she plays and the mischief she gets into. Some label her a poltergeist because, unlike most ghosts, she moves things around and opens doors and turns lights on and off. She displays a curiosity about the newness of the building. Instruments kept at 863 Music, run by Danny Mastrodonato, are strummed by unseen little hands trying to learn to play the guitar.

Tiffany Thamer Phelan of the Phelan Paranormal Group has looked into haunted places throughout the state and offers the group's services for tours and investigations. She has been to the Heard countless times and always knows something is going to happen.

> *There is also definitely poltergeist-type activity that happens at the Opera House. I was actually just there a couple weeks ago during the day, just for fun, and my daughter and my friend who came to investigate with us saw a chair on the stage moved several feet to the right.* [They also saw] *a very large projection screen, about the size of a king-size sheet, fall over onto the chair. These items were several feet away from each other. The*

Opposite: The haunted Heard Opera House, also known as the Arcadia Opera House.

Left: Do spirits walk these stairs at the opera house?

> *air-conditioning was not on, and there were no windows open. We were literally the only ones in the Opera House.*

Especially now, Agnes loves the room where she is said to have died. The energy there is just different, and the constant parade of little children coming in and out provides her plenty of company, even if most of them don't know she's there. Most.

The room is currently occupied by Prism Studios, run by Danielle Wells. She claims she knows there are several spirits in the room where she conducts dance classes for the youth of the area. In fact, she feels what she does actually makes the activity increase. "Agnes is really excited about the kids being here. When I first moved in, she would trip my air-conditioning. They said they used to play pool in here, and that [the air conditioner tripping] would never happen." Danielle has felt the presence of the little girl and maybe caught a glimpse or two of her in the mirrors around the studio. She feels the music and energy generated by the kids is inviting and reminds Agnes what it was like to play with other children. Most of her classes are focused on bringing out the best in the children, and that kind of caring and focus may be attractive to a child who cannot leave this world. Wells did not know about the reputation of the room when she began renting the space, but she has never felt scared or intimidated by Agnes or any of the other spirits at the Opera House. "I've always felt comfy energy. It seems warm and inviting, even when I am here by myself."

Agnes is still careful to stay away from the window. The story goes that Agnes was invited, along with many of the other children from the local orphanage, to attend regular movie screenings at the Heard Opera House. One night, she and a few friends became bored and decided to tour the rest of the building, eventually settling on the corner room because it had windows on two sides, so they could see the lights all up and down the street. Here is where the story splits. Some say Agnes and her friends were fooling around and she slipped and fell out the window. In another version, she accidentally broke the window and had her throat cut by the shattered glass. Others say she was leaning out, admiring the lights, when she slipped and fell. Then there are the darker stories that speak of her taking her life or a group of bully children forcing her out.

In any case, Agnes is said to have fallen and died. For more than a generation, people have seen her at the window. People on the streets also see her. One report describes a woman driving by and seeing the little girl in the window. She sat and watched her for so long that cars began to honk at her to move through the light. For reasons that change based on who's telling the story, a rosary has been nailed to the outside of the window. It may be to bless Agnes or to keep her inside the building.

There is another story told about her death. This one explains why there are other children seen and heard in the building. Businessman John Heard bought the property in October 1905 for $2,000 and wanted to install a bank. These facts are true. There was an orphanage on the property, a total misuse of prime real estate, so Heard decided to start a fire to get them out of the building. He miscalculated the damage it would do and did not know there would be kids in the building when he torched it. Arcadia burned and the children died, trapped and screaming. These facts are not true at all. Heard did benefit from the fire overall, creating several new businesses before leaving town less than a decade later. This has led his name to be attached to many of the ghost stories told about the Opera House and even

An outside view of the window from which the young girl is said to have fallen, complete with a rosary hanging outside.

to the idea that he remains on-site to pay for his sins. But no children, Agnes included, died in that fire.

What more evidence do you need for the existence of a curse than the fact that Arcadia, in some weird ways, defines itself by that tragedy that happened there more than one hundred years ago? Like many small towns in

Florida in the early part of the twentieth century, Arcadia was experiencing a little bit of a boom thanks to industry and railroads. Another trend struck as well. On November 30, 1905, Thanksgiving Day, a fire raged through the streets of downtown, razing all but a few buildings in the area. The cause of the fire has changed over the years. Most people cite a match discarded by a man trying to light a cigar or pipe while using an outhouse. Others have said the fire was set by some local bankers and shop owners who were looking to cash in on their insurance or make a new start of downtown with their own stores and businesses. One of the most infamous versions of the story, the beginning of the first of many rumors to become fact, for some, over the years, is that the fire was started by the women of Arcadia. They had grown weary of their husbands and sons going out, so they set the bars on fire. Before they could stop it, the blaze was raging out of control.

An odd thing happened after the fire. The concept was echoed in article after article at the time throughout the county, state and country. Reporters picked up the story in newspapers all across America. They spoke briefly about the impact of the fire, never mentioning whether anyone had died and rarely mentioning any of the people who had gotten hurt. Even accounts of the damage to the city were given quickly so the larger themes could be explored. Time and again, reporters instead talked about how the fire was the best thing ever to happen to the city and how it was going to make Arcadia stronger. At times, it was compared to a forest fire that must burn away the dead wood so the forest can survive. This moment, many said, would show the true character of the townspeople as they rebuilt Arcadia into a better community. The *De Soto County News* even went so far as to joke, only weeks after the tragedy, that it was bad enough they had to deal with the fire, but now the carnival was coming to town. While this idea seems inspirational at first, the lack of empathy for the actual tragedy and the near-robotic way it was repeated come off as more sinister than comforting or encouraging, like the fire was meant to happen. In fact, many feel the history of the city began on that day, and the lack of official paperwork from before Thanksgiving 1905 has forced historians to rely on oral tradition.

No orphanage stood at 106 West Oak Street where the Heard is now. No children died in the fire; no one died as a direct result of the fire. No fire ever burned down the buildings on West Arcadia Street.

Another story may have evolved from the facts getting in the way of a good backstory. A man met a young girl at the orphanage. As she grew older, he began to fall in love with her. Whether out of guilt or rejection, he took her to the Heard and killed her, trapping both of their spirits there. Some assert the man was actually John Heard himself.

If you believe the stories, Heard was a busy man. "There is also the spirit of Sarah, who is Mr. Heard's mistress," says Tiffany. "She was pregnant, and the story goes that Mr. Heard decided that he was going to stay with his wife instead of going with Sarah. She hung herself in the rafters on the stage while she was pregnant." She and her team frequently capture Heard's voice on tape, answering specific questions about himself. He does not tell them which version of the story is true or why he may be trapped there. They also get pictures of Sarah hanging from the rafters.

Tiffany lists her experiences there without hesitation.

> *I've been touched several times. We hear disembodied voices. Literally nobody is in the room or even the whole opera house but us, and we all audibly heard a voice. We've caught shadows on camera of apparitions. People have physically seen shadow figures moving, specifically in the back hallway. We have motion detectors go off when there's nothing there.*

That leaves just Agnes and the other children. The orphanage in question did reside in the town but was almost a mile away and on a different street. Known as the Florida Baptist Orphanage or the Florida Baptist Children's Home, it first started housing children in 1904. It occupied eighty acres of land with eight buildings (later reduced to six) and looked to "maintain, support and educate the indigent white orphans of the state of Florida, irrespective of their religious creed or nationality." Basically, according to Spessard Stone of the *Tampa Morning Tribune*, the center was designed to take in poor kids from the area and find them Christian homes around the county until they turned eighteen, given they could prove their father was dead. It was moved to Lakeland in 1948. It is hard to tell if any of the original buildings remain. There is a church there now and what seem like the foundations of old buildings nestled away in the middle of the neighborhood. While it is impossible to confirm if any children died there in the forty years it was operational, people believe the land where it once stood is still active. There is a small playground there now, and people walking by have seen kids playing on it only to find them not there when they look back. Small shadows run around the plot of land. Some in the neighborhood talk about loud giggling and screams coming from that area. Some hear knocks on their doors when no one is there. Laughter is heard moving around the corner of the house, but no children.

The neighborhood where the old orphanage once stood.

If you walk the neighborhood, you'll notice something odd, and once you see it, you can't unsee it. An unusual number of houses have doors and windows painted light blue. The house will be one color with blue trim around the entrances, usually clashing with the color of the main building. In the South, there is a tradition known as haint blue—an accented version of the word *haunt*. The belief is that if you paint the entrances of your house or the roof of your porch, it confuses the spirits. They think it's water and will not cross it. True Southerners go one step further and place jars outside the house. The puzzled ghosts get trapped and travel into the jars. Dump them every so often, and you'll keep your place from ever getting haunted. It makes you wonder why so many buildings in that area all are painted the same color blue, especially when many of the houses look run-down and uncared-for but have a fresh trim of haint.

Tiffany may have other proof that something happened to at least some of the children from the orphanage.

> *We do also find that once in a while other spirits will kind of be drawn in and be there for a little bit. Then they won't be there anymore at all. I think the energy of the Opera House kind of draws them into the area, and they want to check it out.*

This would make even more sense if they went on field trips to the Heard on a regular basis and had fun watching movies and playing.

That might be enough to explain the hauntings, but Danielle doesn't care too much about the backstory. She just like having Agnes around.

> *She's really excited about the kids being here. At the beginning of the summer, they put a show on in the auditorium of all children. There's this chandelier that no one has access to. It just does its own thing, whatever it wants. They say it happens whenever there is a show or a band she likes. The children were performing, and it lit up.*

What more evidence do you need?

CHAPTER 3

THE CHILDREN ARE PLAYING IN ARCADIA

Imagine closing your eyes and counting to ten. You hear a rustle of leaves and even a chuckle or two from a child as you make your way up the numbers. Finally you shout out, "Ready or not, here I come." Shadows seem to scatter behind stones, and balls of light flicker and go out. The Richardson children are ready to play. You stroll around, carefully listening to any sound that might give away their position. You tiptoe to the nearest tree, hoping to see one of them nestled in the crook, but when you jump out, there is nothing there. You heard someone behind there; you're sure of it. For a moment, you're caught up in what you're doing. You forget the playground you're creeping across is a cemetery and the children you are looking for next to headstones and behind trees have been dead for sixty years. You forget but then hear a whispered snort behind you and turn in time to see seven balls of light darting away, jumping over each other and spinning before disappearing again.

You walk back to the Richardson children's graves, seven simple headstones lined up begging to be taken care of and for history to be remembered. You realize you will never catch them because grabbing the ghost of a child is like trying to get a headlock on a dream or hug smoke. You also realize the toy truck you placed on the short stone wall that separates their plot from the rest of Oak Ridge Cemetery has moved to the other end. The stuffed purple elephant you carefully placed on top of Vanessa's grave has been stolen and is now on top of Dianne's. Then you understand you are so far in the back of Oak Ridge Cemetery that if they decided to turn on you, no one would hear you scream.

The talking statue in Oak Ridge Cemetery. It's said that it can tell you your future.

But that's not what the ghosts are known for. They love to play. "Now it's your turn," you say, starting to back away from their graves. If they play fair, they won't look as you hide, but they always catch you. You sit by the bench near the water with your eyes closed and wait for that familiar tug on your shirt telling you that you've been caught.

All seven of the Richardson children died within twenty-four hours of each other, poisoned. It was big news back in late October 1967, especially when the focus of the investigation moved away from their babysitter, Bessie Reece, to their father, James Richardson. James made little sense to those who knew him. He was known to spoil the children, often sneaking them treats and asking his boss at the citrus grove to set aside money so he could afford to buy his older kids bikes for Christmas. Reece, on the other hand, had more direct access to the children. She was also on parole for having killed her husband with poison. Richardson had recently taken an insurance policy out on the children, one that had not even been processed yet, and after several searches, the police mysteriously found a two-pound sack of parathion, an insecticide known to be highly toxic, in his shack. The authorities' minds were made up. The whole thing was a mess, and Richardson was sent to jail. It was not until 1989 that he was exonerated and released from jail. He tried for the next few years to get the money he felt the state owed him. He also was taken advantage of by those who used his case to profit, but he was never able to receive the money he deserved. He eventually died in 2023, far away from his children's graves.

The kids are alone, but not really. They have each other. Oak Ridge Cemetery has its share of ghost stories, well known to the citizens and paranormal investigators. You have Talking Mary, the statue who guards the Hollingworth plot. She has been known to speak to people who turn their back to her and ask for guidance. There are stories of kids having whole conversations with her, saying her voice was coming from the statue. They were told to come back again sometime to chat, which they often did. There is also the memorial to the British pilots who lost their lives training to be part of the Royal Air Force. They traveled to Arcadia and Clewiston, unable to train at home due to the frequent bombings by the Germans. Those who died in accidents and by friendly fire are buried at a monument in the middle of Oak Ridge. When you walk among the neat rows of headstones, you notice that all sound from the outside world goes away. You are in a vacuum. Over the years, people have heard and seen old fighter planes overhead that go behind a cloud and never come out. The Union Jack is meant to be flown at all times. People mourning at the cemetery or just enjoying the peaceful landscape will see it one moment, and then it will be gone. They'll look back again a few minutes later and it might be flying at half-mast or flowing at full.

The Richardsons are sometimes lost in the mix. There are definite sections to the cemetery, and each has a different feel. Being in the way back

The graves of the Richardson children at Oak Ridge.

against the fence and close to the back entrance might be perfect for the little ones. It allows them to play undisturbed. Night falls, and the orbs of light appear. They are different sizes and colors, some the size of golf balls, the largest bigger than a grapefruit. Most are white or yellowish, but people have also seen green and red and blue. One person spotted a purple one. Maybe children from other parts of the cemetery see what is going on and come along for a playdate.

The balls of light run into each other, as if they are playing tag. They swirl around each other like they're dancing. There is a small stone wall, no more than six inches high and mostly sunk into the ground, that sections off their plot. The spheres slowly float over the barrier, moving an inch at a time. You can almost imagine a young child, arms outstretched, trying to walk toe to heel across it without falling. Then there are the times they just hover in the air, four or five at a time, as if they are staring at the people watching.

They want you to join in the game.

Not too far away, in another part of Arcadia, three different children play their own game. For as long as people have worked the groves, they have known you get out of there before the sun sets. Like they're in a scene from a vampire movie, they move a bit quicker as night comes on, not needing to check watches or phones but knowing by feel that something is changing around them. They don't linger and tell jokes. The mood is not right for that kind of thing. Sometimes they challenge each other to stay just a bit longer: your manhood is measured by how long you're willing to stick around. If you really want to show them, you actually wait until dusk, open up the new gate, walk right up to the graves of the Lott children and stay in Coker Cemetery long enough to see if the children are going to come out that night. Very few do that, but enough have to keep the story alive and to keep it spreading. Arcadia has many urban legends, but the story of the Lott children is, among certain people, more than just a story told by a campfire. It is their alarm clock.

The Cokers, it's said, sold their land a while back to the citrus growers, who plowed through what was growing there and replaced it with oranges. As they worked, they discovered a family burial site. Unable to move it and ethical enough to not just plow it under, they planted around it and kept the headstones and bodies intact. Over time, grass and weeds took over most of that part of the field. You couldn't see the cemetery unless you were right on top of it, but everyone who worked there knew where it was. Murmurs had already started among them that the land was cursed somehow, and when it got dark, the bad spirits would float over the graves in the form of dull balls of light. If you stayed there, they might possess you.

Those who were less superstitious told a slightly different story. There was nothing evil in the cemetery. It was quite the opposite. The lights were the spirits of little children, babies really, and they were lost. They had been buried and dug up and moved, and their family was far away. They could not find their way home, but they could play with the other children buried there. And they could play with each other.

If you can uncover the GPS location of Coker Cemetery, and if you trust that a cemetery is there even if you can't see it, you can watch their games. You park and walk in a straight line and take a leap of faith. Ignoring the snakes that the area is famous for, you continue until you come over a hill, and you immediately see the chain-link fence, a recent addition from the town and the historical society, and the sign telling you you're in the right spot. The best time to go is an hour before the sun sets. It takes a few minutes to get out there, and you want to settle yourself. You need to experience how quickly the atmosphere on the other side of the fence changes. Then three balls of light, about the size of oranges, rise from the ground. Some see them in different colors, most often blue and red, but most say the orbs are a dull white. They come up to about chest level and then spin around each other. They leapfrog. They spin and approach the gate but never cross it. Children should never go outside without an adult.

Above: The hidden Coker Family Cemetery.

Right: When the sun sets at Coker, the children come out.

Three little graves and three balls of light confirm those spirits are the Lott children—for most, at least. The fact that they are not Cokers, the only people interred there who aren't, confirms for many why they are there. No one can remember, however, how the story of the curse came about, although it is told as if there were written records of it.

The Lotts owned the smaller farm next to the Cokers. They were experiencing more success and expanding their crops and even expecting their first child. A little while before the baby was due to be born, a man, sometimes identified as a "gypsy," arrived in a broken-down car and asked if there was any work to be had on the land. The Lotts arranged for him to stay and get paid by the week, with no commitment to stay. For that first week, he slept in the house, had his meals with the family and worked relentlessly next to Mr. Lott. Some of the harder land was tilled for the first time, a new fence was built in one area and large stones were pulled from the ground and set aside. At the end of the week, the man told the Lotts he would be moving on and asked for the money he was owed. Mr. Lott refused, insisting the man had eaten his food and was given shelter for the week and that this was a fair exchange for his work. The stranger demanded he get what he was owed. Mr. Lott pulled out a shotgun. If the man had a problem with the arrangement, he was more than happy to go into town and talk to the local law. He was sure they would side with him.

The stranger walked back to his car. Right at that moment, Mrs. Lott, who had taken a liking to their new worker, came out of the house holding her belly.

"That baby will never see its first birthday. And no child you bear will ever make it to the age of one." With that, the outsider tipped his hat sarcastically, got into his car and tore down the dirt driveway.

Mary was born a few weeks later, in 1916. The family was so happy that they pretty much forgot about the curse. Four days before her first birthday, Mary mysteriously died. Nellie was born a few years later, in May 1920. She passed away in early April 1921. Then Freida Mae came, and she was the light of the Lott family. Even as a baby, she showed an energy and grace they had never experienced before. Her first birthday hung over the family like a dark cloud, but when it came and went and nothing happened to their little angel, they thought the curse had been lifted. Then, five months later, Freida Mae died in the night. She was buried next to her sisters.

The Lotts knew the only way to break the curse, or even just to live in peace, was to move away from Arcadia. They abandoned the farm and the little graves marked only by the stones the stranger had pulled from the

Left: The grave of Mary, the first of the Lott children to meet her fate.

Right: The grave of Freida, last hope for the hopeless Lott family.

ground. The Cokers took over the land. They took pity on the children and moved them into their family plot, maybe dooming them to an afterlife of imprisonment.

That is where they still lie. And sometimes play.

Another odd legend has grown up around the Lott children, maybe started by the superstitious people working the groves. They say if you place a coin on each of the Lott children's graves, it can break any curse placed on you. Leave a coin and get good luck. There is no pat on the back or voice saying the curse has been broken or good luck will come your way.

It's a leap of faith.

CHAPTER 4

HOLIDAY AND THE GHOST PANTS

One of the most unusual ghost stories in Florida takes place in the small town of Holiday, located not too far from the bustling center of Tarpon Springs. To tell the story the way Laurie Champion told it requires a bit of context and an understanding of the area. That's all an outsider is allowed: a little understanding. Pasco County likes a good ghost story, and some areas, such as Tarpon Springs, embrace and even celebrate the haunts that draw people to the seaside town, almost as much as its Greek culture and world-famous sponges. Holiday is not like that. The townspeople hold their secrets close to the chest and rarely allow others to know about them. Laurie Champion was guarded like that as well, and it may have been the fact that she was born outside the area that allowed her to open up a bit about the haunted pants, the cursed area around Holiday and a cemetery that is either the reason for the weirdness or another of its symptoms.

If you consider Tarpon Springs the center of that area, then Holiday and the mysterious area near it named the Anclotes are its suburbs, even though they are not technically in the same county. Not that Tarpon Spring doesn't have a haunted history of its own. Halloween might be the only time the old ghost tours pop back up now, but there was a time when the shopkeepers and restaurant owners up and down Dodecanese shared their tales with tourists. It seemed every store had some kind of spook associated with it, and ghosts were part of their business.

Tarpon Springs, maybe the most haunted town on the Gulf Coast.

The most infamous of these remains a part of the culture of downtown. There could be an entire book dedicated to stores that sell soap and have a problem with the other side, but the most well known is GetaGuru at 777 Dodecanese Boulevard. The actual address is part of the aura of the place. While it's a total coincidence, many have crafted stories about how it was either cursed or blessed by the numbers, citing numerology and mystic connections. The soap shop, which is often referred to by its old name, the Sea Horse or the Sea Horse on the Docks, was originally opened in 1934 by William Poulos as a curio shop. According to the shop's website and author Kimberly Rebman in her book *Haunted Florida*, Poulos was well respected in the community and was actually known as a healer of sorts. The stories vary, but it is said he was a guru himself or had been a guru in a former life.

While the tale has been changed over the years by retailers and online retellers, some aspects of it have remained the same. Two lovers were kept away from each other and were destined to find each other. The man made his way back to Earth, but she was stuck on another plane and needed to be brought back using ritual and a strong belief in love. Certain ceremonies allowed her to come through and find true love, but they left a hole between the worlds that workers and customers still feel today. They say one section of the store just has its own energy. Thing that are kept near it have a tendency to come up missing. Then there is a darker side. Rebman writes that Eleni Poulos, William's great-granddaughter, who runs the store, once had a painting she had done sweat its color when placed near the west side of GetaGuru. She sometimes feels watched or sees dark shadows and even once saw a woman manifest there. Books and other merchandise get moved around.

Nearby Rose Cemetery has a bit more of a sinister past. Some consider it a dark mark on the community and have worked for the last few decades to change what was done wrong there. Originally, it was called Rose Hill, and urban legends say it was deep in the back of the beautiful Cycadia Cemetery. Back then, it was illegal and considered bad form to have African Americans buried in the main parts of the burial area. Eventually, Jasmine Street was created to completely separate the two. Cycadia became the jewel of the town, and Rose was left uncared-for and vandalized. Today it is better tended, but the damage may have been done. The cemetery is said to be home to countless lost graves; some are marked only with wooden crosses. Many of the tombstones are damaged and worn. Some have even been cast aside, their original plots lost to time. Most do not go there if they do not have to, leaving it in the hands of historians looking to keep the old spirit of it alive and paranormal investigators looking to just keep up with the spirits.

There is an animalistic growl heard at night. The cemetery itself is closed after dusk and well looked after by the local police, who have reported hearing the sound themselves during their rounds. Most say it is a dark energy that has been known to psychically and physically attack people who stay there after dark.

But Laura Champion held her adopted home, Holiday, as the better place to live than Tarpon Springs. When she talked about the ghostly pants people see there, there was always a sense of delight. She was a leading authority on the ghost stories of Pasco County before her unfortunate passing a few years back, and the story of the pants was perhaps the most unique and closely held one in the area. In Holiday, people do not talk to outsiders about their ghosts. They have been burned too many times. They look down on ghost hunters and investigators who want to spend time in the cemetery and the vandals and careless teens who think mixing beer, trucks and ghosts is a good

Above: GetaGuru, also known as the Seahorse.

Right: The door said to be a portal to a different dimension.

thing. Citizens within the community would have their own experience and then remain silent until they heard someone else start to talk about a similar one. It was a badge of honor to see Holiday's spirits, as if in so doing you were somehow being given a blessing and becoming part of the town. In what may be the most haunted part of the state, home to the most closely held secret in the paranormal world, stories of phantoms are commonplace but best left untold. Maybe that is why it is so hard to know if Dr. Seuss ever heard them.

When Laurie first moved into town, she was not sure how her neighbors would take to what she did in her spare time. She had spent years looking into the supernatural and had already started to gain the respect of the paranormal world.

> *When I first moved to this neighborhood, I kept a low profile. No one even knew I was a ghost hunter for ten years. Over those ten years, I heard lots of stories from neighbors about strange happenings, and since my ghost-hunting pastime became known, I have heard endless reports.*

She witnessed too many dark figures in the woods near her to count and recorded hours of voices on tape not heard in the moment. Holiday was the perfect place for what she did. There seemed to be ghosts around every corner.

One story, above all, stays with her.

> *About twenty years ago, I went to a barbecue at a neighbor's home, a fisherman who had lots of local buddies. Someone started telling a story, saying he had seen a pair of pants with shoes, like a man from the waist down, run across a nearby road on a rainy night. Another man jumped in to say that he saw it, too, and pretty soon they were comparing notes. With all I have seen and heard myself, I chalked this up to just too much beer and a bunch of tall-tale fishermen telling yet another ridiculous tale.*

It would be easy to call the story a great legend from a small town. It has that feel to it. Legends, however, are usually the work of hearing that a friend of a friend of a friend heard something. While many accounts came secondhand, enough people saw the mysterious pants over the years with their own eyes to make the story ring true, even if it remains unexplained. Laurie continued to learn details from people until she had her own experience with the unusual ghost.

About two years later, I was coming home from a friend's home. It was late, and it was raining; there was a slight fog but nothing blinding. I saw my neighbor's eighteen-year-old son on the side of the highway near the road that leads to my road. His motorcycle had broken down, and he was soaked to the gills. I picked him up to give him a ride home as he lived four houses down from me.

We were driving down the road that eventually dead-ends to my road, and as we came over a rise and into the dip that followed, I could not believe what I saw. I was driving my old Bronco, which was very tall, and I had my high beams on, which illuminated the road for quite a distance. There are no streetlights, and the road is very dark at night. The rain was still coming down but only a light drizzle compared to the earlier downpour. There, about thirty yards in front of my truck, was what appeared to be a man from the waist down, crossing the road into a nearby trailer park.

The ghost had no upper body. There was only a pair of pants, suspended in midair. The clothes matched the description given by the men at the barbecue. "The pants were brown, uniform-style pants, with shoes and a belt, but there was absolutely nothing visible of the man above the belt. I locked my brakes and sat in disbelief and looked over to the boy beside me. He looked scared to death." The youth asked her if she had seen what he had seen. "I said that of course I had, and he replied, 'I am so glad. I have seen it before, and no one would have believed me, so I never told anyone.'"

The experience made Laurie more open to legends and local folklore.

That evening, I learned that no matter how ridiculous something sounds to me, I have to give the benefit of the doubt to people. I have heard several bizarre claims since. I can honestly say that even though I scoffed and shook my head when I heard the tale, I now have to eat my words on the ghost of the traveling pants. I have no explanation for what I saw that night. I haven't seen it again, even though others claim to have.

There's one possible reason why the ghost is only seen from the bottom down. Laurie was a firm believer in some of the science of paranormal investigating, including ideas gathered from different religions. In later years, she spoke of the idea that the soul is located near the heart and travels directly to the brain. If a spirit is at peace, those parts of its spectral body may fade first, leaving only the lower part of the body, which will follow shortly after. There is an odd logic to that, but reports of ghostly

The intersection where the ghost pants are seen.

pants are limited in the paranormal world. If her theory was true, they would be walking on every back road in America. It also does not account for the ghost being seen for decades.

It may have been that idea that appealed to Dr. Seuss when he wrote the book *What Was I Scared Of*, published in 1953. It tells the story of a young boy who sees a pair of ghost pants near his house and tries to hide from them. There is a path and a pair of pants; the details match. It is such a unique story that he had to have been inspired by the haunting in Holiday, but there is no evidence he ever visited Holiday or overheard the tale during a visit to Tarpon Springs. Seuss had a habit of not talking too much about the inspiration or meaning behind his work so readers could explore their own ideas. Laurie was never able to date the ghost story, although she believed it went back generations, so maybe tellers were inspired by Seuss.

The other thing Laurie never commented on was who the man might be or where he was headed. This was not a case of ignorance. Instead, she may have been protecting the cemetery the ghost was roaming toward. If you draw a straight line down the street from the ghostly pants, you come to Anclote Cemetery, and anyone living in that area is right to be aloof. They all know it's haunted, and they all know they want people to stay out. Over the last few decades, people have been attacked by unseen hands there but have also damaged and abused it. The cemetery's story is much like that of Anclote itself.

Anclote is considered the oldest place in Pasco County, having been founded in 1867, almost a decade before Tarpon Springs. The town grew slowly, adding more houses and fostering its own sponge business. It did not have the urban appeal of its neighbor, and when the railroads decided to run through Tarpon Springs instead of Holiday, the town began to fail. Fires in the early 1900s added to its decline. It became a good place to live, an underdog, and inspired fierce loyalty in its citizens.

Jack and Tom may have been among those early citizens and may be buried in Anclote Cemetery. Residents are buried there for free, and the earliest headstone dates to 1871. No one knows Jack's and Tom's exact histories, but things have been pieced together over the years. Tom may have been a pirate who was caught trying to steal from the town. It has a long history of defending itself against bandits and a long history of hanging them. Tom is seen hanging from a tree close to the edge of the woods, swinging like a smudge of black in the dark. He moans and cries. He may be the man the locals call the Hobo. That ghost is seen walking down Calvary Road, smelling bad and following people who walk near there at night, his head cocked to the side.

Jack is believed to be a Civil War veteran. He is dressed in an old military uniform, although locals believe he could also be the Dark Man seen in the cemetery, a figure seen as nothing more than a thick black silhouette, devoid of physical features but moving like a person. During the day, Jack lurks by headstones or walks the rows, reading the names. If they approach him, people will hear a loud laugh behind them. They turn to see nothing there, and when they turn back around, Jack is gone. He has a reputation for not liking women. Ladies visiting the graves are often pushed or feel like someone is trying to grab them by the throat. That kind of anger is what makes people believe that at night, Jack stalks interlopers who try to enter the cemetery in the form of a thick black fog, solid and capable of physically assaulting visitors. If you are a citizen of the town, you're safe. All

Above: The Anclote Cemetery, with the woods in the background.

Opposite: The road where Cindy is supposed to walk.

others need to be on guard. He is also said to be the source of the inhuman growling that comes from the trees beyond the cemetery, warning people not to dare come in.

And with good reason. Over the years, Anclote Cemetery has been wrecked by people. Headstones have been vandalized and knocked over, and people have driven their off-road vehicles through it and turned up the dirt. Locals keep where it is as hidden as possible. They patrol the road leading to it, taking down license plate numbers and stopping people at night, asking what they are there for. Back in the day, they created an informal block patrol to look after the dead.

Even they have a hard time explaining exactly who Cindy is, although they have put together some details they think fit. Her story, spread through Internet posts peppered with information given by psychics and ghostly voices on tape, has never been confirmed. It's so oddly specific that it feels as if it should be true. She was a young lady who spent her time at the

Anclote River Park in the 1980s, known by locals as the Moon. It is unclear whether she was attacked there and then brought to the cemetery, but the legend says that she was attacked by four men who sexually assaulted her and killed her. She has most often been seen in Tarpon Springs on Anclote Road in a pink halter top and jeans, but she is associated with many spots in the area, including the local power plant. Often her throat is sliced and bleeding as she begs you to help her. Other times she is physically fine but scared and crying.

She hitchhikes the road, sometimes being picked up and sharing parts of her story before disappearing. She then follows people home. She is not confined to that road, though. Cindy has been seen up and down the two-mile stretch between the Moon and the cemetery. Some believe her body may have been dumped there. That is where she approached several young ladies and told them about being hunted by the four men. The sheer number of places her ghost is seen, sometimes stumbling, sometimes running into the woods, makes it feel like more than an urban legend. Cindy is a perfect example of how haunted that area is and how the ghosts defy what we think of the supernatural.

She's the perfect partner for a pair of pants walking down the road in the rain. In Holiday, those kinds of stories make perfect sense.

CHAPTER 5

HOW MANY BODIES ARE IN THE ROAD?

"It happened all the time when I first started," says a local tow truck driver who frequents McGregor Boulevard while making nightly runs. "It was just between, like, 10:00 p.m. and 1:00 a.m. I started and thought it would be a good place to hang out and wait for calls. I could get anywhere from there." Being new to the area, he had no idea what a weird reputation McGregor Boulevard in Fort Myers has. The first few nights, the lights inside the truck would shut off or flicker. He lost calls, and then they would pick up when he moved off the street. "At first, I'm thinking bad Wi-Fi area, right? Then I'm noticing as soon as I'm off McGregor, everything is perfect. If the lights didn't shut off and everything, I'd just say bad signals. Can you explain both happening—and only there?" He now parks his truck at the Edison Mall a few miles down the road.

There's something there you can't quite put your finger on at McGregor, and it's usually so subtle you don't think about it until you hear someone else say it, too. You're in the city, though. Calls shouldn't drop. The internet should be fine. Your car shouldn't lose power. You shouldn't see ghosts.

It's one of the busiest streets in the city during the day and early evening. It leads you down the backbone of Fort Myers, with direct connections to the Edison and Ford Estates at one end and the beaches at the other. After midnight, the traffic that almost defines the street is almost nonexistent. The houses and estates are still there, but they lie dark and dormant. Maybe that is why seeing the little boy walking on the side of the road is so unsettling. The drivers, and it's almost always a couple, stop and ask the boy if everything is okay.

"I'm trying to get home. I live down the street."

The little boy is offered a ride and gets into the back seat in tears. As they drive, he begins to calm down, sometimes talking about how long it has been since he has been home. The car travels on; the boy begins to get excited and jumps up and down in his seat. Finally, he shouts out that his house is coming up and demands the driver stop. They do, but when they look back to let him out, he is gone. This is a classic urban legend spread in just about every town in the country. In Florida, similar stories are told about Tiger Trail Road in Dunnellon (there, you might accidentally pick up the main villain from *Jeepers Creepers* or a black-eyed kid looking to steal your soul), the Old Dixie Highway in Ormond Beach and Rolling Acres Road in Lady Lake. The story is so familiar that it rings true because you've heard it somewhere else, but it also sometimes convinces people that there is nothing going on at a location. *I've heard that story before,* they think, *so everything else must just be a story as well.*

Above: The haunted McGregor Boulevard.

Opposite: The stretch of road where the little boy is seen.

Then the story changes, and you're forced to change your mind.

There is another traveler on the road who is a bit different. Drivers on McGregor Boulevard between midnight and the witching hour of three o'clock encounter a tall man lurking on the side of the road. He is not walking on the easily accessible sidewalk but slightly in the driver's path. This is right after a small bridge and a slightly sharp turn in the road, so if the driver is not paying attention, they could easily clip the man as the turn is made. Even though there are streetlights, he appears to be surrounded in darkness, as if he is not really there. As the driver approaches, their headlights don't hit him. No light seems to touch him. The driver comes up next to him, and he disappears. He does not jump out of the way or turn to walk out of the road. He just vanishes.

One of the more common experiences on McGregor, and the one that you may overlook until you start to hear others talk about it, is like that of the tow truck driver. McGregor can be a dead zone for electronics. Certain parts of the road play with lights and car systems. The radio may malfunction, switching through channels and even producing voices not

coming from stations. GPS systems and phone applications spin with their "rerouting" message or shut off. Satellite radio does not respond. A similar thing happens hours north of Fort Myers on the infamous Interstate 4 as it travels west out of Orlando and into Daytona—an area referred to as the I-4 Dead Zone. There, the unexplained activity has been attributed to the construction plowing through a cemetery near Sanford to make way for the road. McGregor shares a similar origin story, although the details of the dead have changed over the years.

Tootie McGregor, an influential woman in Fort Myers, was tired of having a cow road outside her door. She also wanted easier access to the business ventures she had her hands in. She promised the city she would pay for a road to be widened and extended from Whiskey Creek to Punta Rassa. The city agreed. A construction engineer named Maurice Pearl was brought in from Benton Harbor, Michigan, to handle the design of the road and oversee its construction. After planning where the street would be laid down, he set out to find stones and shell. His intent was to create macadam, a type of concrete layered with rocks, shells and other natural ingredients that forces water not to be absorbed but to flow off the main pavement. That would be perfect for the strong rains of Southwest Florida.

Pearl sailed across the Caloosahatchee River to a small island near Matlacha Pass. It was not much more than a patch of land in the water, too small and too lacking in resources to sustain life and positioned in the perfect spot to act as a bit of a dumping ground for tides and storms. There would be plenty to harvest there. As his crews began to dig out the shell from the mounds, they discovered something else barely buried in the sand and sediment. As reported by the *Pensacola News* a few days later, "At about 9 o'clock Wednesday night, while the gang was working by firelight, one of the [workers] struck into the shell bank with his pick, and was surprised when a human skull rolled down the bank at his feet." That day, eight human skulls were discovered.

What happened next set off a firestorm of controversy. The crew continued to dig and found more bones. According to the *Pensacola News*, "The bodies were all facing the river, and were apparently buried as they fell, without any regularity. No arms, ornaments or jewelry were found, the only thing in the nature of implements being an old broken jar clasped in the arms of one of the skeletons." If this happened today, the whole site would be shut down and an investigation would take place. It wasn't quite the same situation in Southwest Florida in 1913. At the time, progress was being made down both coasts, and ground was being broken. Many knew they were hitting important archaeological sites, but there was not too much concern about that. Progress had hit Florida, and any place south of Tampa on either side that was near a beach was going to be developed.

The bones themselves offered little explanation of what had happened there. Many of them were so old and frail that they turned to dust as the workers were digging. Others were whole, and Pearl sent them off to the Smithsonian for a possible explanation. According to the *New Press* at the time, "Some lie flat on the face; others prone on the back: some have arms extended: Some bodies are at right angles to each other; some are piled in a heap." No positive identification could be made of where they had come from. The Calusa were mound builders, but local authorities looking over the remains Pearl sent them said the features did not match any known tribe and were almost definitely European. The number of bodies has changed over the years, but the most consistent number published after the events of the dig is 103.

Various theories have come up over the years. Some believe the whole cast comes from one of Gasparilla's ships. In the 1800s, the infamous pirate had a skirmish nearby. This theory is somewhat misleading: it came from a work of mainly fiction written about a man who did not really exist. Another theory is that the remains are those of pirates, but for a different reason. Pirates did not bury their dead with their loot, and they did not drop most of them into the water. They did not want a curse to fall on either the loot or the water. Instead, they would make landfall on small inland islands and bury their dead in shallow graves, as was part of their code. They would mark these places and spread word to others about them so other pirates could utilize them and everyone could be sure not to go digging where someone else may have hidden their treasure. Ships would anchor nearby, send a small boat to the place marked and unceremoniously cover their men, careful not to anger any of the ghosts that might be hanging around. Pearl had found one of those spots. After all, the island is known as Sword Point. What better name for a pirate graveyard?

The best answer might be even more simple. Sword Point is one of many small islands nestled amid larger ones, such as Sanibel, Captiva, Matlacha and Pine Island. It is essentially a net, catching anything the tide wishes to leave. Over the years, many people have died near the water in storms and battles and accidents, and their bodies were never recovered. A rational explanation may be that the bodies washed up on the island over time, and any seemingly rational placement came about by chance. Science was not nearly advanced enough at the time to date the bones or tell if there was any relationship between them. It is just a case of the fate of the waves.

The construction crews and their bosses did not care too much about where the bones came from. Many of the bones were dust and could not be sifted from the sand, rocks and shells. Others had melted into the environment through the heat and weather of Southwest Florida. Pearl took

The turn in the road where the Dark Man most often walks.

what he wanted, including the bones, and continued the project, laying the bones of 103 people to rest in the road in front of Tootie's house.

The curse those pirates looked to avoid may have fallen on the people of today.

The story does not end there. While Maurice Pearl comes off in some accounts as having somewhat enjoyed the notoriety of the entire incident, in real life the whole job left him with an uneasy feeling. He was never fully on board with disturbing the graves. It is also said he encouraged local officials to erect a monument to those who were originally buried there, a request that has never been answered. He went back to Michigan and was said to be troubled by what had happened. Some say he even went insane. One day, he walked out his front door and was never seen again. There were no sightings of him, and no body was ever found. He just left his house and slipped off the face of the earth.

All that is left of him is the road he helped build, some lonely souls walking the road and the rumors of a curse.

CHAPTER 6
THE CALUSA GHOST LIGHTS

Legend tripping is a time-honored tradition. To some, it means learning as much as you can about a tale told about a location, sometimes with a ghost and sometimes without. You try to figure out why these people told the story this way at this time. Then you go out and experience the story just the way it is told: experience over evidence. There is an older definition, though. Imagine that one creepy house in the neighborhood, the one everyone in town knew was haunted. You would challenge one another to knock on the door three times to prove yourself. Or maybe it was that spooky cemetery where an old man was seen. You'd have to place the school flag on his grave by moonlight. Then there were the popular spook lights. Teens would flock to places like Oviedo or Ormond Beach to sit and watch the lights and maybe make out for a bit.

Southwest Florida has its own version of those lights. Catching the Calusa lights on Burnt Store Road in Cape Coral used to be a popular thing to do when nothing was going on and you were miles away from the action of Fort Myers. "It used to be called the Grandstands," says Lee Ehrlich, founder of Ghost Pro and a respected paranormal investigator, about the patch of concrete by the side of the road. The grass has taken over most of it. Ehrlich lives next to the location where the lights are seen. "In the 1960s and 1970s, they used to sit on the paved section of the road and watch the Calusa spook lights down the street." According to Ehrlich, the lights came out almost every night back then and always baffled the people who gathered to watch. They would watch them float back and forth between the swamp and woods and the road, about the size of the headlights on a train.

All that remains of the Grandstands, where teens used to hang out waiting for the Calusa ghost lights.

It's important to know what they were watching and where they were looking. In theory, a ghost light or orb is the concentrated spirit energy of a person who has died, although Ehrlich and others are open to other supernatural explanations. Some believe they could be extraterrestrial, not necessarily aliens from another planet but just something not understandable that does not exist in nature. Another popular theory is that the orbs are elemental, like fairies or demons.

The area we are talking about is a neighborhood on the border between Lee and Charlotte Counties. Burnt Store Road is a bit of a misnomer; the lights are seen in an area bordered by Old Burnt Store. It runs only a few miles from the waters of Pine Island, Matlacha and any number of little islands. It is a marshy area, somewhere between a forest and a swamp: classic Southwest Florida. It's the kind of place wild hogs used to call home during the dry seasons and alligators familiar with slightly salty water still like during the wet months. You can imagine what walking through this part of the state was like before people came in and began developing. In fact, despite recent development of Cape Coral, this part still feels a bit desolate. It was even more so fifty years ago. The houses almost seem like they are the element that does not belong, and in some ways they do not.

Kids would come out and watch the lights at night, not wanting to be the first one to leave and miss something. Ehrlich has spoken to enough of his neighbors to understand what it was like back then. "It was a neighborhood thing to do. None of these homes were here. This is where kids would come to party. It was like Inspiration Point." The lights themselves were unpredictable. Sometimes they would meander through the neighborhood, stopping at houses as if they were trying to see who was moving in next door. Other times they would almost get impatient, fly into the air and travel across the tops of the trees. "Some kids would get curious, and they would venture deeper to follow them."

That "deeper" is the only place the lights are still seen, and they are still seen. Traveling out there is like inviting a light show. Sometimes they are off in the distance, almost like they are on the nearby shore. Other times they come right up to you, sizing you up. They tend to follow rough paths cut into the swamp during dry times. That's when they are not soaring into the trees.

Ehrlich and other investigators continue to go out and track the lights, usually choosing to enter the marsh through the nearby Charlotte Harbor Preserve. They also know other spirits may stand close to the ghost lights.

> *I'll see them, sometimes the size of a softball. They'll cruise the tree line and then shoot like a cannon a half a block and then appear again. Every time we come out here, it's a little bit different. Sometimes it's a shadow form, sometimes it looks like Slender Man, and sometimes it's just a white light. It's always unusual, and it never fails to produce.*

The ghost lights are not the only thing unusual about the area, one that Ehrlich knows well. He says many of the houses nearby experience all kinds of hauntings, and most residents have lived there long enough to know their environment. They are not scared by strange noises in the night. "There used

The entrance to the Charlotte Harbor Preserve, the easiest place to view the lights.

to be the ruins of an old weigh station here that took trucks. There was an old legend of a boy walking across the street. We don't know what happened to him." Several people have talked about seeing a little boy walking in that area who seems out of place and not quite there. There is some distance between houses at that location, and a broken-down weigh station is not a place for a kid by himself. Drivers say they will focus their attention on something else for a moment, and the little kid will be gone. Ehrlich said he

One of the many "clear spots" in the swamp where the lights dance.

would try to send drones past the old building, and they would not fly over. They would just stop and hover, like they had hit a wall.

Whatever the lights are is the center of the energy there, and there are many theories about what they might be. The most obvious explanation is that these lights are the souls of Calusa who died in the area. The Calusa were the Spartans of old Florida. They were said to be taller and more muscular than Europeans and the surrounding tribes. They were primarily hunters and gatherers, living off the natural resources around them but not farming or keeping animals. They were fierce. It was widely said that they practiced human sacrifice, killing prisoners and members of the tribe as a way to appease their gods. It is said they fought off Ponce de Leon, inflicting the wound that eventually killed him. De Soto himself decided it was better to head north after meeting with them and hearing rumors of their power.

The Calusa were not immune to war, and they suffered major losses from disease after their meetings with the Spanish. They were mound people, creating massive piles of shells and stone, and would often use some of these to bury their dead. These were upset as development of Cape Coral rolled through the marshes. While some remain and are preserved, most were destroyed and the bodies displaced. Now imagine that the majority of the preserve leads directly to the ocean. Tides and storms can be devastating to the area, unearthing bodies and sending those lost at sea onto the land. That coast would catch all, and over time, who knows how many corpses were lost in the muck? Any one of these could account for wandering souls.

The Seminoles might offer another explanation. The first Spanish fort was built not too far from Old Burnt Store, but it kept getting destroyed by storms and the Calusa. It was pretty much abandoned, but as Florida became a state, another was constructed on the same spot, which eventually became more of an outpost with a store. The Seminoles in the area made a tentative peace with their neighbors, but things became strained, leading into the Seminole Wars. The tribe in the area was led by the famous Billy Bowlegs, who could see the turn things were taking for his people. He led an attack on the outpost, burning it to the ground and giving the road its name. The soldiers in the area counterattacked, killing many of the Seminoles who were fleeing into the wetlands nearby. Legend says they refused to allow their enemy back into the area to recover their dead. The bodies just sank into the swamp and mud. They were not given a proper burial, and their souls are now forced to walk the area looking for their bones.

The Calusa believed that every person had three souls inside them, and when someone was sick, one of their souls had escaped and was roaming. Souls were drawn to the woods and water, perhaps as a way to reconnect with the spiritual forces that lived there and strengthen themselves against the ills of their bodies. A shaman was needed to track the spirit down and force or scare it back into the person's body. If not, they would die. Now imagine what someone from the tribe would think of all the sicknesses the Spanish brought with them. They were dying in record numbers with no way to bring that third soul back from the woods.

One last idea is that the lights are actually *tei pei wankas* or *tai pei wankas*. These are the ghost lights reported by Native American tribes all across the country, many of whom speak of them in connection with small, hairy men of the woods known as Pukwudgies. While primarily a northeastern United States and southern Canada legend, these three-foot-tall creatures are known by many different cultures throughout the world. The name *Pukwudgie* has been adopted by numerous tribes across the county. Regardless of the name, the small monsters themselves are known more by their deeds than what you call them. They are tricksters at best, violent and cruel at worst. There are tales about them kidnapping the young and burning villages. They would lure people in the woods, mainly men, using the tei pei wankas to attract and seduce them into coming closer. These lights are said to be the souls of people the Pukwudgies killed.

I had been researching Pukwudgies in New England for about ten years when I relocated to Florida. A year after the move, a friend of mine messaged me about a case he was working on. Knowing I had been tracking reports of for years, he wanted my advice about a woman who was experiencing them close to Boston. He did not know that I was no longer in Massachusetts. This woman had been experiencing Pukwudgies ever since she was a child. Usually they pop up to warn you to stay out of the woods and swamps they call home, appearing several times in your house to get the message across. I had never heard of one returning decades later. She first saw them in the swampy areas near the new development she was living in. They stared at her, smiling impishly, and then ran off, disappearing after a few steps. She saw pairs and groups of them in those days, but when they came into her bedroom at night, it was always one at a time. They would stand at the foot of her bed or near her window, looking very serious, and shake their finger at her before fading away. Sometimes, there would be several glowing lights in her room when this happened.

My friend said she grew up in this obscure town in Florida I had probably never heard of called Cape Coral. He laughed when he said the name of the road she lived off as a kid, some weird name like Burnt Store Road—about two miles from where I was living at the time.

Ehrlich and the people he investigates with are open to any of these explanations. They know the Calusa lights are more about the experience than about understanding. They still come to the preserve, discussing what has happened to them in the past and knowing the chances are good something new will transpire. Usually the lights are passive, if not curious. Once in a while, they go off script and feel a bit more threatening.

The three of us were out walking around. In front of us was this big arcing curve in the path. We see this bright light following the curve. It's coming at us in a threatening way. The three of us are not ones to turn and run, but we felt like it was time to go back to the car and maybe get a gun. As it's coming, it's evening our speed. Then it starts to double its speed, and the ball is coming at us. We started walking faster, almost at a run. It was faster than us at a run. It got pretty close and then zinged off into the bushes like they always do.

Every once in a while, the ghosts need to push back against their guests. Ehrlich also knows he does not need to be in the preserve to see them.

Me and Josh were coming back one night from one of our spooky trips. We see this glowing light floating about thirty feet in the air. It's like two in the morning. We get out, and it's in the street right in front of us. Most times it's about the height of the street signs, but sometimes it will skim the tops of the trees.

Not everything associated with the Calusa lights is an actual light. One night, while scouting around Burnt Store for a documentary he made about the phenomena, Ehrlich encountered something a bit different.

We were down where the single lane becomes two lanes. I was walking, and I heard something. I had my guard down because were in the middle of the street near one of the only streetlights around here. There was this thing. It looked like a werewolf. It was walking like a racoon with a hunched-up back, but it looked canine, with pointy ears and a pointy snout. It was probably about two hundred pounds. Diana yells out, "What the hell is that?" because it came out of the shadows into the light. When she yelled that, I lit up my light, and it ran into the bushes.

Ehrlich knows the area well enough to understand and recognize the natural beasts that live there, and he's experienced enough to understand when something just doesn't feel right.

That line gets blurred in Cape Coral. People new to the area will laugh off the idea that a haunting is living next to them but become amazed by the history that the ghost stories force them to remember. Maybe that is what the lights have wanted all along. Their ghosts open up the narratives of their lives to be remembered.

CHAPTER 7
THE FISHERMAN AND THE PIG

Alice Cheney was an outsider. That's the only reason anyone outside of Collier County has ever heard her story. It was buried deep in a Michigan newspaper that no longer exists, sandwiched in between advertisements for men's formal suits and a letter to the editor about a local traffic issue. The fishermen most directly in the path of the ghost of Virgil Weeks forgot the name and forgot the story, for the most part. Boats steered by younger men avoid the area more by tradition than for a specific reason, scratching their heads as they try to remember precise details their grandfathers may have passed down to their fathers. They just know they don't fish near the Death Trestle, an odd name given that there is no trestle bridge anywhere near the stretch of water leading into Marco Island. That bridge was taken down years ago.

Fishermen tell plenty of stories. They talk about the biggest catch they have pulled in and the much larger one that got away. They don't tell too many ghost stories. In an area rife with tales of pirates and ships lost at sea during storms, you would think they would be on the front lines of spreading those legends. Sometimes their superstitions sneak through, but they only pass their ghost stories among their peers.

But Cheney was an outsider. She was a character in her own right, a former female world record holder for catching the largest shark. She came to Florida to test a new way to lure the fish and was forced by a storm to spend time in Naples and on Marco Island. In the early 1940s, Marco was the Wild West, unsettled and mostly wilderness. She decided to spend time

The Judge Jolley Bridge, which replaced the old railroad trestle bridge.

on the water despite the warnings of the men around her to stay away from where the train bridge met the island's shore.

About an hour into her journey, Virgil came upon her. She noticed him off the bow of her boat. He was walking toward her, no more than fifty yards away. His hands were stretched out to his sides as his toes skipped over the surface of the water. The clouds appeared to swirl around him. A pulsing green light surrounded him, and he got close enough for her to see his terrified expression, as if witnessing her was frightening to him. She began to lose her breath. When he was almost close enough to touch her boat, he opened his mouth. She recalls sensing he had something important to say. Instead, the screech of a pig at the slaughter came from his mouth.

Anyone who spends their time looking into modern ghost stories is confronted with an honest truth: true crime and the spooky go hand and hand. Many of the creepy places of the world trace their origins to unsolved mysteries or tragedies. Even in Florida, activity at places like the Devil's Tree in Port St. Lucie and the screams from the woods at Rolling Acres are attributed to Florida's most prolific serial killer, Gerard Schaefer. The Chi Omega House on the campus of Florida State University is haunted by Ted Bundy and one of his victims. According to urban legend, on the night of his murder spree there, one of the murdered women came back as a ghost and woke up her roommate to help her safely get out of the house. If a ghost story is built on the most infamous thing that's happened in a place, murder and crime are easy explanations for anything paranormal that might happen there.

If you travel to Marco Island from Naples today, you will most likely cross over the Judge S.S. Jolley Bridge, sometimes called the Judge Bridge by locals. It is really one of two ways to get out there. The overpass that stands there now was built in 1969. It replaced a slightly older one and was named for a man who presided over the county from the bench between 1935 and 1959. Before that, the Atlantic Coast Line Railroad, also known as the Acline, ran out to Marco across a trestle bridge. Where it made landfall, there was a little tender house off to the side to maintain the trains and take care of an occasional boat that might need some under-the-table work.

This is where Virgil Weeks and his friends decided to set up shop one afternoon and get drunk on cheap wine. He was twenty-five, his friends not much older, and they had spent most of the day fishing nearby. The water was good there, and a professional could make a decent day's pay working the water. William "Conch" Sawyer and his friends had spent most of their day doing just that. When the group got to the tender house, they asked if

This area, known as the Death Trestle, is where the ghost of Virgil Weeks is said to walk on the water.

they could tip a few back with Weeks and his friends. Weeks agreed, and the two groups enjoyed the late afternoon together. At some point the men began to gamble—some say they were tossing dice—and an argument broke out. Weeks took out his gun and fired a warning shot at the group. Conch fled the scene with his friends but quickly realized he needed to go back and get his equipment. He had leased the gear and would be on the hook if he could not recover it. Before sailing back, he and his friends stopped to pick up some guns, and then they returned and demanded their tools. Weeks refused and threw his jug of wine at Conch, who responded by shooting and killing Weeks with his shotgun.

And here is where the story gets weird.

Conch and his men took off, leaving the dead body behind. Marco was pretty much wild and untamed at this point, so Weeks's friends needed to return to Naples to get the police. They did not want to move the body, so one of them stayed while the others sailed off. A guard was needed because Marco was known at that time for its amazing fishing and its hordes of wild pigs. The group had already seen some starting to peek out of the thick grass, smelling the blood. The man left behind had done his share of drinking that day and then knocked a few back to honor his fallen friend. He passed out. He was woken by the sound of hogs descending on the body. He took aim at the largest and killed it, scattering the rest.

Conch Sawyer was eventually caught, tried and given a death sentence. There are many reasons the living give for why a soul becomes a ghost. Finding the point in this story where Weeks became trapped on this earth is a question of belief. Maybe it was the desecration of his body. About a year later, Sawyer's new lawyer demanded that Weeks's body be dug up so they could prove the shot inside of Virgil was not the same kind of shot Sawyer had in his gun that day. The coroner exhumed the body and performed an autopsy while rain fell. Almost one hundred people looked on, including Weeks's wife and family. According to the *News Press*, the coroner "pulled apart the ribcage and probed into the moldering flesh until he came up with a handful of big buck shot." He continued to pull piece after piece out, examining each one, clearly visible to the onlookers. Conch was not exonerated and remained in jail.

Maybe Weeks's ghost didn't find peace because no one knows quite where he is. After the autopsy, his body was recklessly put back in the grave without much concern. In fact, if you look for his grave today, you will find the headstone lost in the roots of a tree. Most believe his body is not underneath it.

Then there is the injustice that concludes Sawyer's part in the story. Judge Jolley, the same man the bridge is named after, would reduce his sentence to life in prison a few years later. Conch was instead paroled in 1958, but he was immediately back on the police's radar. On his release, for reasons no one is quite sure of, he made his way to the house owned by Weeks's family and threatened them. He was arrested again a few hours later and placed in a Collier County jail but escaped, sawing his way to

The discarded headstone of Virgil Weeks in the Marco Cemetery, hidden now near the trunk of a tree.

freedom. He was never seen again by authorities. Weeks's killer never saw the true justice he deserved.

That's not the story the fishermen told, though. Defiled graves and injustices are one thing, but they knew the true reason their old friend trolled Death Trestle. When Weeks was shot, his soul rose from his body and remained in the area. When the pig was shot, its spirit rose up and possessed the ghost of poor Virgil Weeks. Confused, he roamed the land until he reached the water but was unable to cross. If only he could get passage on a boat—a loophole in the belief that ghosts can't cross water. So that's where his ghost remains, walking the water, begging to sailors to ferry him across but unable to get a ride because the only voice he has remaining is that of a screaming pig.

That is the backstory Alice Cheney was told when she saw Weeks. Then she was told about the *Vigilance*, a tender boat that often stocked up at the little shack on Marco. Only a short time after Sawyer had his sentence commuted, the boat was seen on fire at the Death Trestle. The men themselves had all jumped over the side and were hauled into another boat while trying to swim for the shore. It was not the fire that sent them into the water. They all said they saw a glowing green ghost who "looked like a human but made noises like a hog." When a fire suddenly started without warning, they refused to fight it and fled the evil spirit. When encouraged to go back and examine the damage done to their tender, all the men refused. They said it was bad luck to return. They had noticed the man floating onward and screaming to them. This was now Virgil Weeks's water.

That's the way it remains to this day. Commercial fishermen may not still utter the name Death Trestle, but most keep the tradition alive. Fishermen are superstitious people, even if the reason to be superstitious has been lost. They avoid the area for reasons of tradition more than fear, but every once in a while, usually over drinks, someone will mention seeing a man on the water. Oddly, they say, knowing no one will believe them, he seemed to be shrieking like a pig.

CHAPTER 8

LOVE AND DEATH AT THE TRESTLE

She comes out of the woods—out of nowhere, it seems—dressed in white, as so many ghosts are. There is an eerie green glow around her. She is almost dancing across the tracks, the water below just far enough to make falling dangerous, even deadly. Then you realize she is not dancing but rather floating in the air, her feet moving but not actually touching anything. You also realize the dress is a bit too elaborate to be merely a fancy dress; it is a wedding dress. The moon, often said to be a full moon, clouds over, even though there were no clouds moments before. Then, as she gets closer to where you stand on the bridge in the dark, you also notice her lips moving and the noose around her neck. "Where is John?" she asks, and you are too scared to tell her that you are not sure, but you believe he died over one hundred years ago and is not coming to meet her. She would not listen to you anyway. People have been trying to convince her for more than fifty years that John is not coming back. She never listens.

The story of Martha and John is pretty much forgotten now, but for decades, the ghostly legend fueled trips out to an abandoned trestle bridge in the middle of nowhere in a town that has become not much more than a ghost town. Boyette, Florida, remains a town in name, with about six thousand people calling it home, but it has largely been skipped over and forgotten except by the locals. Most of them do not remember the story of the doomed couple or the bridge in the woods where their story plays out. There was a time, however, when the thing to do on a Friday night, especially when it was Friday the Thirteenth or a full moon, was to stroll a darkening path into the woods, make your way over the abandoned railroad tracks to the edge of Fish Hawk Creek, dare to walk onto the old bridge and wait for John or Martha to make themselves known.

The story starts over one hundred years ago; some tellers date it back even further, to the Civil War (a time long before Boyette was around). John was coming back from the war, making his way back to the woman he loved. As he crossed Boyette Bridge, his horse was scared for some reason. He was tossed off the bridge to the rocks and water below. Martha, who had waited patiently for her man to get back from the fighting, was devastated. She walked from the farm her parents owned to the bridge. She sobbed his name and hanged herself from the same spot from which he had fallen. To this day, her ghost returns, still wearing the white dress she put on to impress him on their reunion and still cursed to wear the noose she used to take her life.

Seeing the two lovers was an event for decades, and people's continued Friday night walks to the bridge at Fish Hawk Creek changed the story. In later versions, John was not coming back from war but traveling across the bridge for his wedding to Martha at her parents' big farm. When he was thrown from the bridge, he was in his best suit and she was in her wedding gown. After he was buried, she tried to move on but could not. One Friday the Thirteenth, she slipped on her wedding gown, convinced that if they died in the same place, wearing the clothes they were to be married in, they would somehow reunite. It was not to be. Why else would they both be seen on the bridge like two different movies playing on two different screens, and why would Martha continue to ask, "Where's John?"

There seems to be two different kinds of ghosts there. John is seen riding his horse along the bridge. People have spoken of also smelling the horse and hearing the sound of hooves on wood. Then they hear the loud neighing of the animal in distress and a scream as they witness the man flying over the railing. Both man and beast disappear, and right after, there is a splash in the water below. No one has ever reported interacting with John or any deviation from what happens. He is what people might call a residual haunting, a recording playing over and over with no hope of getting out of the loop. He is also the secondary character in his own haunted legend. Martha is the one people come for.

According to multiple articles published in the *Tampa Tribune* and the *Tampa Times* in the 1970s and 1980s, legend trippers would travel to where Boyette meets Bell Shoals Road, turn onto Boyette and drive a bit before parking their car at the old tracks. Back in the day, they would be greeted by Floretta Cox sitting on her porch. Old message boards said at one point,

An old cartoon showing the impact of the urban legends about the bridge. *Courtesy of the* Tampa Tribune/Tampa Times; *used with permission.*

the spot was so popular that her family even sold lemonade to those looking to see the spirits. They would then walk through the woods to the bridge and wait for John or Martha to show up. Witnesses to the ghosts say you never see both. Over the years, dozens of people saw at least one of the two, enough of them that it became a thing to do on Friday nights, especially on Friday the Thirteenth, and an excellent date idea for the full moon.

Martha is the subject of so many of the rumors of the story. She has gone from being a woman in distress who takes her life in grief to a tormented bride cursed to walk until she can reunite with the man she can never find. One person speaks of her coming from the woods down a path now taken back by nature and lost, while another person says she comes floating out of the water. One person swears she killed herself at exactly midnight, and therefore, that is the only time to go. Another says the hanging happened at sunset as she was convinced that would be the key to unlocking their new life in death or because she refused to spend another night without him. There is, of course, another version that speaks of John killing Martha when he returns from war and finds she has not been faithful. That version of the story always sneaks in when the real names and the real story cannot be found in newspapers and old books.

That is not the only way Martha's story has changed. One ritual that gained popularity for a while involved some well-known urban legend tropes. You could walk out to the middle of the bridge, turn your back to where she is supposed to come from and close your eyes. Slowly whisper "I know where John is" three times, and Martha will touch you on your shoulder and ask for the details. If you tell her he can be found in heaven, she will tell you the name of your true love. If you say nothing or try to turn around, she will scream and vanish. This version of the tale involves a single man—and it has to be a single man—going out there by himself. The good news is that this can be done any Friday at dusk. You do not have to wait for a full moon or an unlucky day.

No one can trace the story back to any actual people, which should be able to be done. The town does not have a long history, and Martha is said to be part of a family that owned a large farm right over the bridge. There are even those, quoted in newspaper articles, who claim someone they knew was familiar with the family, but even these witnesses cannot recall their name. There is mystery in the town. Like so many other small rural settlements, it rose and fell with the railroad. It had pretty much died out by the time the news articles were published. By that time, the story had outlived the town. Adding to the mystery and atmosphere of the legend, both bodies are said to be buried in the town cemetery, which no one can find. People who spread the story of Martha and John speak of being able to break the curse if they could find their graves and somehow bring the two souls together. At the very least, this might solve the mystery of the lovers' true identity.

There are other ghosts said to be on or near the bridge as well. A man died during its construction and is said to be heard screaming at night. This man could be the John spoken about in the other stories. A teen also crashed his dune buggy by the bridge in the 1970s, and people who knew him are convinced you can see him riding around in the nearby woods and vanishing without warning. None of these have captured the imagination of the community in the same way the couple has. That makes sense, though. The tale of Martha and John has everything a good ghost story needs. It's a tale of haunted love that you could witness and maybe even be part of. It has a creepy deserted bridge and different versions to connect with in case you like your spooky stories a certain way. It even had, for a time, at least, a good glass of lemonade to go with it.

CHAPTER 9
DON'T DARE GO TO MYAKKA

The man has no head. To understand why so many stories are made up about him, you have to know that fact. It's not a trick of the light or your imagination. He's missing his head. During the day, that makes his walks across the road stand out. There are always people walking back and forth across the road at the Myakka River State Park in Sarasota, especially in the winter and early spring. If it were not for the man's having no head, campers and visitors would not even blink, just slow down like they often do while traveling down the road. At night, there is something even more sinister about it. He seems lost, although there is clearly no expression on the face he does not have. At night, he stops in the road, making you brake. He even begins to walk toward the car, waving his hands around furiously. Drivers don't know if it's a threat or if the odd look on his face is something more like confusion. If only he had a mouth to tell you what he needs from you. But the man has no head.

Myakka River State Park (and be sure to use the full name, or you're someplace different all together) has become a magnet for urban legends, although no one can quite explain why. It's an unassuming place no different than others across the state that seem to exist to preserve the natural environment in the midst of pressure to develop. It all might start with Skunk Ape, Florida's version of Bigfoot. There were rumors of his walking around the park, in perfect balance with the deer, coyotes and alligators that call the park home. Surrounded by construction and houses, the state park does not seem like the ideal location for the beast. This is not the Everglades

Big Flats, home of the Headless Camper.

or the Ocala National Forest. But in 2000, a woman sent a letter to a local paper complaining about the cryptid and offering visual proof of the monster, and it launched a firestorm. Debate raged across the cryptozoology community over what it was and whether the whole thing was a hoax, but enough papers covered it and recycled the story that the picture she included became famous. Books published about cryptids usually tend to include it, and it made Myakka River the place to go to see Skunk Ape. According to an unnamed ranger, "They've shot movies here and TV shows, but I don't know a single person who's seen it. They just brought a whole bunch of noise about it, and when it shows on TV, the park will get busy for a while about it."

People continue to hear knocking on trees throughout the park, a theoretical way skunk apes communicate with each other, used by many cryptozoologists to track and get in on their conversations. The knocking has even been known to follow people as they travel throughout the park. Are they being followed by multiple skunk apes, or are the skunk apes telling each other to watch out for *them*? The animalistic growls, the horrible smell and the knocking get worse throughout the night. Other have seen a smaller version of him, almost like a skunk ape child. Some have put forth the idea that this may be something known as a Pukwudgie, a mystical troll-type creature mainly from Wampanoag folklore (see chapter 6). *Pukwudgie* is something of an umbrella term used by many different tribes across the country for their hairy little people of the woods, and there are at least a dozen different locations across Florida where people have seen them.

The man with no head doesn't care about Skunk Ape, though. People have laughed off reports saying he just wants some sugar. He's always seen near the Big Flats Campground about halfway through Myakka. In season, it's one of the busiest of the hidden places where visitors pull up their trailers and RVs to spend a few nights. During those months, you can find people gathered around the fire in the middle of the cul-de-sac getting to know each other, while all around people sit in chairs playing cards and having a few beers. There's a rustling in the woods around them at times, but there are so many animals, it's easy to dismiss. As it gets later and people retire to their camps, the man with no head is sometimes seen by the fire, like he is trying to get warm. He rubs his hands and hugs his shoulders and could be mistaken for a regular guy with his head hung low, out of view. He then expresses a supernatural sense that he is being watched, quickly gets to his feet to reveal he has no head and bolts for the woods that lead to the road.

Toward three o'clock in the morning, he is more likely to be seen stalking around Big Flats, slightly crouched as he is trying not to be seen. He does not show the same aloofness when he knocks on doors, raps on windows and scratches on tents. Campers will come out to check and see what the noise is all about, and he is gone. It could be anyone, except for the laugh. The noise comes as if it's right in front of you, but there's nothing but darkness. When staying for a few days, people will often put up Christmas lights. He does not like these. There will be a noise, and people will, again, come out to check. They'll see the shadow of a man with no head just casually walking away on the other side of Big Flats.

Some people think he may be a Vietnam veteran. For a time in the mid-1970s, Myakka was a popular place for these men to visit. One such man returned to his hometown of Sarasota after serving two tours. It disturbed his family how distant he seemed, and despite attempts by friends and family to console him or get him to talk, he would smile weakly and say he was fine. He wasn't. He had heard of people returning from Korea and shell-shocked soldiers from World War II going to Myakka, and one night, he went to camp there alone, saying he needed the open air. Instead, he snuck into the Canopy Walk, one of the most popular attractions at the park. He climbed both sets of wooden staircases until he could see tops of the trees before him,

The road next to Big Flats where, the lore says, the Headless Camper tries to fish or just wanders.

some one hundred feet in the air. He was dressed in his formal uniform when he jumped to his death.

The story made the news, and it seemed to strike a chord with others like him. People came from all across the state to the location, like they do to the infamous Aokigahara Forest in Japan, to take their lives at the bridge. Some jumped, while others hanged themselves from the side of the canopy itself. It got so bad that the state thought about closing the bridge forever.

Except none of that ever happened. The Canopy Walk and its supports were not built until 2000, long after the Vietnam War and half a century away from the rumors of people coming home from Europe. While there are no official reports or newspaper articles documenting this spot, some people in the community remember hearing it somewhere. Jackson Millen, a resident of Sarasota, has heard the story—but always with the suicides involving jumping. "I don't remember when I heard it. But they jumped from the bridge after coming home." While he admits the story was passed along to him recently, he is sure of the time frame for the deaths.

The fact that there are facts does not take away from the ghosts at the Canopy Walk. People like Jackson Millen have talked about seeing men walking up the stairs behind them and then never witnessing them making it to the top or going down. There will be the sound of boots on wood, slowly walking up, but it's just footsteps. No one is there. "I was at the canopy part looking down," says Millen about one of several encounters he had with spirits there. "I was looking down through the mess that's there at this short guy. He wasn't wearing a uniform or anything. He looked right back up at me. He didn't have eyes, just these sort of lights coming from where his eyes were supposed to be." Millen says the man frowned at him, started walking toward the staircase and vanished when his foot touched him the wood.

Angles on stairs and visitors seen at a distance are one thing, but the Canopy Walk is a straight line. Stepping on it, you get the sense it could fall any minute, even if logic tells you that it is totally safe. Usually people don't walk on it more than three at a time. A woman had just finished taking the first set of stairs and arrived at the Canopy Walk. She noticed a tall man dressed in jeans and an old military jacket standing facing away from her about halfway across the bridge. His hair was messed up and his jeans dirty. He just stood there, not going forward or walking back toward her. This lasted about half a minute, and she began to get impatient. She coughed, trying to politely get the man's attention and ease him on his way. He ignored her. She coughed a bit louder, not wanting to be rude but feeling a bit uneasy. The man was not fully there. She could almost see through him. He slowly

The Canopy where ghostly men climb and disappear.

turned to face her. It was at that moment that some kids began yelling and stomping on the stairs. She looked down at them, and when she looked back up, the man was gone. She crossed the walkway and felt an odd coldness right at the place where she had seen him.

The actual canopy where men jump before disappearing.

The man with no head does not go to the Canopy Walk. In the dozens of reports about the bridge, all those ghosts have their heads. He prefers the road. If he is not strolling curiously through Big Flats, he is walking down the narrow road alongside the marsh. The man has become a legend at Myakka River State Park, a combination of the boogeyman and the Blair Witch, but there never seems to be anyone who has seen him firsthand. He lives within posts on Reddit and ghost story websites, but all those stories are retellings of ones people have heard or read. He walks, he stalks, he warms and he upsets the campers. In almost all the stories, he is active only in June and July, making some people think this might have something to do with his death and why he still haunts the park. Not the rangers there: they laugh when they hear the stories and the supposed date of the man's spooky adventures. They know the park is extremely slow at that time of the year, so slow they actually close Big Flats during those months to campers.

CHAPTER 10

LEAH AND THE GUARDIAN

The ghost of Mary Leah Sandlin has reasons to bawl. Not everyone believes she is the screaming ghost heard at Indian Springs Cemetery in Punta Gorda, but she is the best contender. Some paranormal investigators who have spent time there (Lee Ehrlich, for one) note that the palm trees near her grave sound like a young girl's scream when the wind is blowing. Others point to a suspected serial killer buried near where the shrieks are heard, but this murderer is more of an urban legend. There is probably not a victim of his crimes hovering in the burial ground. The shouts are most likely Sandlin. She is buried nearby, and the moment she is most well known for involved her screaming. She is always said to be the nicest of ghosts in the other location she is said to haunt, benevolent and even helpful. Why would she be called Scary Mary, then? That's not her at all. She does not even like to be called Mary. Insiders know she always went by Leah.

The house where she lived is one of the most haunted in Punta Gorda, some say the whole state. Originally built in 1893, the West Retta Esplanade residence has been the subject of ghost stories since the Sandlins left and the new residents moved in. Through five different families, the stories of Leah have remained consistent, even if the families' reactions to her have changed. James was a former mayor and real estate developer who would eventually establish the cemetery he and his daughter are buried in. His family was hit with several tragedies before he died in 1903, including the deaths of two of his children.

Leah Sandlin's House, where, some say, her ghost travels from room to room. *Picture courtesy of Eve Sylvie Alexander.*

It was Leah's death, which he did not live to see, that gives the house its reputation. She was fourteen in 1909 and was ironing her clothes, using an old-fashioned gas iron, on the porch facing West Retta Esplanade when her dress caught on fire. She began to scream as the flames engulfed her, jumping off the stairs and running down the street. She died of her wounds a few days later.

Since then, she has been a regular at her old house. Several families have gone on the record in books, speaking of invisible footsteps on stairs and across rooms. Different incidents involving Leah turning off irons and stoves in the house make it feel as if she is trying to protect the families who live there. She has also been known to take clothes out of the dryer, maybe not understanding how the appliance works. The porch where the fire happened had burn marks on it for years. People would paint over them, and the stains would reappear. The boards eventually were torn out and replaced, and the spotting stopped.

Evie Alexander is a local writer who has featured the Sandlin House in several of her books and runs a ghost tour through downtown and Indian Springs. She believes it is not just the tragedies that have scarred the downtown area, a place she considers more haunted than the areas around it. She brings up Calusa burial mounds that were destroyed during the town's construction. Maybe the weirdness in such a small area is caused by unsettled souls still on the property.

The Wynn family was vocal about Leah's presence when they were trying to sell the house in 2014. They had lived with her for over a decade and had gotten used to the sounds of her walking and the pressure on the beds the ghost caused when it lay down next to them. They treated her like another one of their children, yelling at her to stop if the activity became too much. The hassle was minimal. When they made repairs in 2005 after Hurricane Charley, Leah stayed out of the new additions. She was unfamiliar with them. Leah is also unfamiliar with Indian Springs, but at least that is where her family is. There is no record of her screaming at the Sandlin House, but the cemetery may be where she plays out the heartbreak of her death.

Not all ghost stories are tragedies. Some are stories of hope and connection and closure. The story of the little lights that flicker at Indian Springs are like that. When you hear about them, and the dark figure who might be protecting them, your heart may drop and then be lifted again. A true ghost story, one that can't be passed off as just urban legend or imagination, should affect you in different ways as you hear it. That's how you can tell it might be more truth than myth. It does not fit a simple story structure. All your emotions get hit, and when that happens, the listener almost experiences the intensity of emotion that might be the very thing that makes a spirit live on after death.

Whether the story of the ghosts of Babyland and their protector is a tragedy or a story of happiness is not determined by the tale as a whole. It all depends on where you are in the story.

This story also starts with James Sandlin. When he donated the land for Indian Springs, he set aside a large portion of it to be used for the children of Charlotte County. He declared that any child who died in childbirth or before the age of three could be buried in that section free of charge. No one is sure when it became Babyland, but it seems to the people in the area that it was always called that. With the mortality rate what it was in those early days of the county, Babyland filled up quickly. There is no way to determine exactly how many children are buried there. You can count the headstones—then multiply that by ten or twenty. For every cracked and weather-damaged marker, imagine five that were stones pulled out of the ground with a name etched on them and another four that were just modest wooden crosses that

Left: Indian Spring Cemetery, home to several infamous Charlotte County ghosts.

Below: Babyland after being damaged by Hurricane Irma.

now lie mostly decayed somewhere in the woods nearby. The number could easily be in the hundreds.

You can hope that children were not buried on top of each other, but these were not the children of people who could afford expensive caskets or were even bound by modern laws of interment. Shifting is inevitable. Care for that section of the cemetery comes and goes in waves. Some will talk about how it lay untouched for decades, the grass overgrown and the stones sinking into the damp Florida soil. Garbage, pushed by wind and rainfall, formed piles near the larger gravestones. Flowers and memorials found their way into the water nearby or the trees. Other times, historical societies or charities or just good citizens have taken over Babyland's care. They have been able to name some of the unclaimed and establish some kind of marker for them. Walking the rows and counting the months in between the birth and death dates can easily lead you to a sense of sorrow. These are the unloved dead.

Now imagine Babyland as the sun starts to set. It's slightly larger than a football field, although it is impossible to say how much of the ground has been reclaimed by the surrounding woods. It is cordoned off with ugly orange fencing, the kind you find warning people to stay away at a construction site. The barrier itself is torn in places and sagging, the victim of Hurricane Irma and Hurricane Ian and the time between them. The sun sets; it's usually one of those Florida dusks that light the sky with orange and purple. Then it is that light darkness that comes with evening. You can still make out the basic shape of things and odd shadows, even when there is no moon. That's when you see the first of the lights, close enough to the woods that you can kid yourself that it's the eyes of the animal in the trees or maybe a lightning bug. Then there are more. Then you hear the first of the giggles.

During the day, people sometimes see little children behind the fence. They shimmer like sunlight reflecting off water. There is something unearthly about them, but at the same time, they are whole. People have called out to them only to be ignored or to see the little child fade away. Cries are even heard. That's not what Babyland is like at night. Balls of light fill the field, floating and darting. It's a light show close to the ground, just about the height of a toddler, and laughs are heard from everywhere. Sometimes one or two orbs glide through the graves, and other nights, the glowing spheres number in the dozens. They are different colors and sizes. It is never the same show, but it always stops people in awe. The cemetery is a cherished spot for local paranormal investigators and enthusiasts, and many report it is the one place they can go where something always happens.

The children are not alone. Leah may be screaming in another section of the cemetery, but Babyland is haunted by something different. Anyone who spends any amount of time in Indian Springs at night talks about the growls that come from the woods. They are guttural, not human or animal but something else that points at the supernatural. Many cultures speak of creatures like ghouls who prowl cemeteries at night, feeding off some spiritual energy of the newly dead like a vampire. There are even reports of shadow figures who observe the living and the dead. They are more likely to appear to watch children and the ghosts of children. The lights go away, and the growls continue.

Or at least they continue until the Guardian comes out. Imagine the stiff back and precision of a soldier walking the Tomb of the Unknown Soldier. He's dark and tall, with no facial features and nondescript clothing. He is almost like a shadow, but those who spot him say he seems as solid as any person and his steps make noise in the fallen leaves and swish when the ground is wet. He starts on one end of Babyland, patrols the outside of the fence, walks almost all the way into the woods and then turns and walks back. Along the way, he may fade out for a few moments and reappear farther down the fence, walking with a determined stride. When he walks—and people spot him at different times during the night—the growling stops and the lights and laughs come back.

The children have a guardian angel watching over them in the night and keeping the bogeyman away.

Who is their protector? There is really only one candidate. It makes sense that a larger-than-life hero who gave his life for the people of Charlotte County should continue to keep watch over its children.

If you stand at the edge of Babyland, you'll see there is only one headstone nearby. If the story of the ghost children makes you feel uplifted because those poor souls have found friends in death, the grave of Marshal John Bowman will have the opposite effect. His grave stands by itself. There are no other plots in the immediate area, and the marker itself was donated years after his death by people he did not know. His wife and the kids he cared for so much in life are buried counties away, a tragic ending for a man who gave so much.

Bowman was brought into Punta Gorda to bring law and order to a town rife with crime, corruption and booze. He was good at his job. In the seven years he served, bootleggers and criminals grew to respect and fear him. There were those who resented him as well. In 1903, he was shot through his kitchen window, a child in each arm and a cigar still in

The grave of Marshal John Bowman.

his hand. His daughter Lizzie's dress was so covered in blood it was used at trial to prove how gruesome the crime scene was. A man named Isaiah Cooper, who had threated Bowman, was convicted of the crime, although very few people believe he actually did it. The real shooter, a man by the name of Dick Windham, is buried less than fifty yards away—oddly, right next to another man he's believed to have killed. Cooper was sentenced to death but eventually had his sentence commuted by Albert Gilchrist, one of Bowman's neighbors and a good friend of his. He eventually escaped a prison work camp.

Bowman was buried in Indian Springs, and his family moved back to Wauchula. He is buried alone, only a short distance from the man who killed him and the friend who allowed his killer to go free. This is the kind of thing that keeps a spirit earthbound, trapped by unfinished business. That is not the story with Bowman, though. The only unfinished business he has is making sure those children near him are safe. He could not protect his kids in life, but with him on patrol, the souls in Babyland can play all they want. That makes his ghost tale more of a love story than a tragedy.

CHAPTER 11

CROSSING THE ROAD AT SAINT LEO

There is a central theme that runs through everything you find out about Saint Leo University in Pasco County. In the last one hundred years, the school has done its best to be part of the community as it works to carve its own identity into the Florida landscape it inhabits. Former students talk about how everyone knows each other or how they could recognize someone across campus even if they never spoke to them. Staff members know the feeling of kinship and family there is one of the things that makes it different from the other large campuses across the state. People from Saint Leo's take pride in having experienced college there. It is no wonder their mascot is a lion.

When it comes to Saint Leo's ghosts, there is a similar sense of connection, although the community part slips away a bit. Students and staff fall into two camps and firmly plant their feet down in them. The first group will tell you they have never seen a spirit and they do not know of anyone who has. They have never heard the stories—and if there *were* stories, they would know, because everyone talks, and the group is small. Then there is the other group. They speak of ghostly monks walking across streets and visiting graves and old housekeepers walking through walls. They say everyone knows about the ghosts and talks freely about them. They would know, because everyone talks, and the group is small.

Saint Leo's is an oddity in its environment. It originally opened in 1889 when a Catholic named Edmund Dunne moved into the area, wanting to establish a more solid foundation for his religion in an area of Florida where

Catholicism was not the popular belief system. The school, named for Pope Leo the Great, who lived and ascended to the papacy in the fifth century, has shifted its educational focus with the times without losing sight of its overall mission. It has been Saint Leo High School and Leo College Preparatory School as well as Saint Leo Military College. It might be this latter incarnation that gives the campus one of its more unique but overwhelming aesthetic qualities. The school does not feel like other campuses in Florida but rather

Opposite: Saint Edward Hall, home to the ghost of Genevieve.

Right: The Dark Man known to disappear and walk the campus.

has the Benedictine feel of a school in New England. The Abbey is the center of campus, overlooking an artificial landscape, but that same area is dotted with wooden buildings that look like they come from a makeshift military base. These are no longer dorms but still dominate that part of campus. There is a statue near the library that also looks out of place and unsettling. It appears to be either a hooded, black monk or the Angel of Death. It was originally placed there as a marker for a time capsule in late 1983 and is said to represent the Benedictine monks who call the campus home. Unlike the friendly statue of Fritz the Lion, it is also said to move around campus and even follow students.

One account on the paranormal website Backpackerverse talks about a student who saw a hooded figure, much like the statue, several places on campus. He was convinced the dark man was following him. He saw him in the library and on the football field as well as in the hallways of the school and several dorms. He did not make the connection to the monk statue and said the dark man seemed to be seen by only him.

While Backpackerverse has been known to exaggerate stories and publish untrue accounts (in fact, there is no football field on campus; the school is dominated by its baseball team), this student's story has been echoed by several others. The most compelling story might be Ted's. He claims he and his friends decided to decorate the statue with a Saint Leo's baseball cap and take some pictures for homecoming a few years back. The next few nights, he woke up to find a smaller version of the statue, minus the hat, standing at the foot of his bed. He was not asleep and could move freely. "I just lay there as that thing pointed a finger at me. It was real. I could hear my roommate snoring and the television on. The second night, there was even a little rain on my floor. It had been raining that night." On the third night, slightly over his fear and just wanting to get a good night's sleep, he apologized for having taken the pictures. The figure never appeared to him again, but all the photos they had taken that day were mysteriously erased from their phones and social media accounts.

There may be holes in Ted's story, but he tells it as if it really happened. He does not know why he was the only one of his friends to get the visits. "It wasn't even my idea. It wasn't my hat. I'm going to be honest with you: I think those other guys saw it and were too embarrassed or scared to say it. I saw the look when I told them."

Another ghost appears in students' dorm rooms but causes much less of a stir. Students living in Edward Hall report that a woman walks through walls and sits on beds. Descriptions of the woman, who is known as Ms. Genevieve, vary dramatically. Some see her as an older woman dressed in older clothes, like ones from the 1950s. Other see a younger woman. This is the ghost people who attended the school talk the most about. They are told about her, and usually they've either seen her or know someone who has.

Gemma Rose is a librarian in the Flagler County public library system and graduated from Saint Leo in 2018. She is a history buff who has also researched the paranormal in her area. She claims most students know about Ms. Genevieve and even offers the backstory people spread:

> *The legend is: Ms. Genevieve was a housekeeper on campus. One day, she was walking the laundry up the stairs and lost her footing. She fell down the stairs and died instantly. A few weeks later, she was replaced by a new housekeeper. One night, on the third floor, the housekeeper was cleaning the bathroom and saw the face of an old woman appear. She got scared and immediately quit her job.*

Gemma also says that people who report sightings of her say they have even heard her humming. While Miss Genevieve seems to not be unhappy with her work in the afterlife, Gemma believes her presence adds to an overall feeling students report in that building. "For me, Edward Hall had the most 'sad' energy walking in. Like when you go to a funeral; it is just a heavy feeling. Edward Hall always felt like that to me." Others say the same.

Meghan Kennedy, who writes for the school's student newspaper, *Lions' Pride*, has mentioned the story as well. In one article, she throws the story out as if anyone reading about it does not need the backstory. They already know it and think that it is true.

Neither Miss Genevieve's existence nor her death at Edward Hall can be confirmed. Some have said the school covered it up to please the other families at the school, an excuse often given in urban legends. The school does acknowledge that the story persists, and while no one is willing to go on the record to confirm any sightings, at least one published report sets it all down. Jane Govoni, Mary Spoto and Valerie Wright, authors of the book *Lions, Leos, and Learners: A History of St. Leo University*, clearly felt that the tale needed to be included, even if it was placed in the same section as a legendary alligator nearby and other silly stories students spread. In a section titled "What's the Buzz," they write:

> *Over the years several students walking the campus in the quiet of the late night have reported seeing a lone figure crossing by a window on the third floor of Saint Edward Hall, once a boys' residence hall. When they have entered the building or reported the sighting, no one was ever found. It's hearsay. Over the years, this same mysterious figure has been spotted crossing the same windows on the third floor of the building. Each time someone has investigated, no one has ever been found in the building.*

In other words, people have reported the ghost, but it acts too much like a ghost for them to be proven right. Ms. Genevieve has also been said to be the woman who sits outside Edward Hall in what is known as the Peaceful Reflections Garden, a Native American medicine wheel formed by stones. Students are encouraged to walk and meditate in it. It also has several benches. An older woman is seen sitting on those benches with her head down and her hands together in prayer. She disappears when approached.

There is another monk who is known to walk the campus, but he never gets past the front lawn. He might be on his way to the abbey from his resting place across the road in a spot called the Grotto. People driving down State

The Grotto across from the campus of St. Leo's.

Road 52 at sunset speak of seeing a man who is usually assumed to be one of the brothers from the Holy Name Monastery on campus. He comes from the woods quickly, almost as if he is running, but his movements are not hurried. The monk steps onto the road. He is wearing dark robes, and his face is covered by the hood over his head. The driver assumes he will stop, giving them the right of way, but he walks across the street as if the car does not exist. The living swerves to avoid the dead, who just continues to walk as if the whole thing has not happened and evaporates as he reaches the front lawn. This has happened often enough that locals drive slowly around dusk when approaching the college.

If those same drivers followed the path the ghost came from, they might encounter a few more just like him, but people of Pasco County and the students at the school do not make a habit of going to the Grotto when the sun is going down—whether out of fear or respect. They know whatever walks there is best left undisturbed at that time. They are even reluctant to share the stories. The spirits, after all, just seem to be on their way to evening prayers, known in the Catholic Church as vespers. These are generally conducted around sunset; bells from the abbey signal when they are beginning. It is a

The grave of Corolus Herricus Mohr, the first president of the college, thought to be the leader of the ghostly monks at vespers.

tradition deeply rooted in ritual, and it may be that sense of ritual that forces those buried at the Grotto to continue the ceremony.

Once you cross the street, you will see a path that seems to lead into the woods. Climb some stone stairs and take a short walk through the trees, and you'll find a monument celebrating the graduates of the college who gave their lives during World War II. Some say that farther into the woods, there is a small, respectful cemetery, but people generally stop at the mausoleum and the open stone chapel. Corolus Herricus Mohr, the monastery's first abbot and president of the university, is buried there. On his grave are the words "*O Domine, quia ego servus tuus; ego servus tuus, et filius ancillæ tuæ*," which means, "O Lord, I am your servant and the son of your handmaid," a reference to Psalm 116. The quote is generally accepted as meaning that the buried person dedicated his life to God. In this case, that may even mean after death.

The path the ghostly monks are said to walk down, trying to get to the abbey.

Around the time the bells should ring and vespers begin, people say you can hear singing at the Grotto. It is almost more of a chant than a hymn or song. The most frequently reported sighting is of one man, thought to be Abbot Mohr, but on occasion, he is joined by several others. Men in black robes, some with hoods and others with their faces clearly visible, come from the burial ground as well as the woods. They walk slowly, in step with each other, their feet hitting the ground but making no sound. They start up the path, joining each other as they travel. If undisturbed, they continue across the street but are never seen crossing the campus or appearing in the church itself.

It is hard to say whether any of the stories from Saint Leo are true or if they're just a combination of religious ideas mixed with urban legends. No one has ever been able record the monks on their way to prayers or the dark man who hates practical jokers. No one can say whether the housekeeper existed; no one has spoken to the woman walking in a circle. College campuses are breeding grounds for ghost stories. These stories help build community and establish traditions and give those on campus the feeling that there is something that unites them.

CHAPTER 12

THE ONE PLACE EVERYONE SAYS IS HAUNTED

If you try to have a conversation about ghosts in Southwest Florida, you may find yourself stretching to get past some of the fancy places that are always listed as haunted. There's a hotel here and there and a restaurant where someone said they saw something and the story gained traction. Much of the reality of a haunt is based on the belief that ghosts are real. You by no means have to think this to enjoy a spooky story, but a true ghost story, one that stays with you once the spooky is over, has to be firmly planted in the understanding that we live on after we die. Simply being creepy is not enough.

Then there are some places that make believers out of people. They visit with no intention of seeing a ghost and no foreknowledge of it being haunted but leave feeling uneasy or unsettled. Those who accept that ghosts are real will retell their experience, especially once they hear other people talking about the moments they had there and the other encounters they've heard about. Those who don't believe in ghosts listen in, making connections in their mind and doubting their doubts.

The Koreshan State Park in Estero is one of those places. Few walk away from visits there *not* feeling that they just had something happen to them. Some can put their finger on it; others explain it away with a laugh but lean in closer to hear what others are saying. Get into a discussion about phantoms in Lee County, and eventually, the conversation turns to Cyrus Teed.

And everyone has a story.

One of several haunted buildings at Koreshan State Park.

Seneca began to speak to George Colby sometime in 1875 in the small town of Pike, New York. Seneca could not be seen—he was, after all, a spirit—but his power was felt. Colby was drawn to leave the state and head south along a trail of energy to start a new spiritualist camp at a source of immense power. It was a strong calling from a deeply spiritual place, and he packed up his mission, with a few followers trailing behind, and landed in Volusia County, Florida. There he set up Cassadaga, or Water Beneath the Rocks, and began what he considered the good work. For the past 150 years, Cassadaga has drawn in spiritualists, the best psychics in the world and people from all across the globe who are looking to get a glimpse into themselves and their future and maybe even converse with the dead. It is now known as the "psychic capital of the world" and well known for its many haunted locations, including the Hotel Cassadaga.

Joseph Smith departed from roughly the same place in Upstate New York in the 1830s and settled in Utah. No one can question the impact and influence of the Mormon Church. It seems odd that the same area would produce such similar yet vastly different groups of followers who then traveled a great distance to set up their thriving communities. A dozen other prophets hailed from roughly the same patch of land and led doomsday cults and radical splinter groups to different parts of the country. Some were seen for what they were, and others still exist today in another form. There must have been something about the area at the time. Cyrus Teed must have felt it himself, and while some of the men who led their flock off into the horizon are still revered, outsiders looking at Teed's Koreshan Unity movement gasp and giggle at it, considering it more a cult than a movement.

But Cyrus didn't. He took what he received in his vision deadly seriously. After having a vision that he was the new messiah, he renamed himself Koresh and began to win people over to his way of thinking. While this summary is slightly reductive and doesn't capture the nuances of what he preached, the basic tenets of Koreshanity call for a belief in "cellular cosmogony," or that the Earth is hollow and the sky we see is just a layer within the earth. Koresh's followers felt compelled to move to Estero, Florida, to set up a New Jerusalem where they could live according to their beliefs and conduct experiments to bring themselves closer to the divine. Once they arrived, they basically carved their settlement out of the swamp along the river and began to construct buildings on their three hundred acres of land. They also established a short-lived balance with the people around them, exercising their belief in communal living by trading with the citizens of Lee and Collier Counties. More than two dozen buildings went up over the years, most of which have been razed or replaced. It was considered a utopia by many given its beautiful surroundings and the lifting up of women as important people within the community, and people from across the country made their way to Florida to join the group. In retrospect, cynics today see it as a cult. There was a charismatic leader who asked you give up all your worldly possessions in exchange for a

The Founder's House.

set of unusual beliefs. That would be too simple a statement to sum up the people of the Koreshan Unity. Teed and his followers believed.

It would be easy to break into a discussion about how the ideas of the Koreshan Unity movement threatened the beliefs of the people in the area or how the influx of people made Teed a threat politically to Lee County. This is a ghost story, though. Put those ideas in the back of your mind, but remember they are just a piece of the puzzle. Teed chose to settle right there, and it was not just because of cheap real estate. There is an energy in what is now the Koreshan State Park that even nonbelievers feel.

"Kayaking. I just went there to kayak and look at all of the beautiful scenery. I had no idea of the history. It was only after I went people told me about the Unity people and the weird things there." Will spent an afternoon at the park sailing down the Estero River and having lunch on the dock that leads up to main buildings.

> *I sat on the dock eating a banana and a tuna sandwich I had thrown in my cooler. I was just sitting there looking out on the water and saw a man across the river. He was dressed in drab clothes, real simple. I didn't look too hard. Then I noticed all of the bird and animal sounds had stopped. I looked up again and saw him, only that's when I saw he was actually walking on the water. Just strolling right above it like it was normal. Then, blink, he was gone. The sounds came back. I took off.*

"People have their own experiences in the park they don't know are paranormal." Nikki Marie has worked as a vendor, a meditation leader and an energy clearer. She was drawn to the park the way many are and walked the grounds knowing many of the people she saw were not alive. "Things are happening right in people's faces, and they don't see it." During reenactments and events, it is easy to mistake a ghost for an actor, something she feels happens there all the time.

There are some moments in the park's history that have to be explored. As more people joined the community, the Koreshans became a threat. The food they supplied, especially the hundreds of loaves of bread, changed the economy of Lee County. While trying to break up a fight, Teed was beaten about the head and took almost a month to die from his injuries. There are many who believe he was set up. Several politicians and businesses owners in the area thought he was becoming too powerful. In any case, after he died, it was widely believed that he would rise again. His followers set his body in a bathtub onstage in what is now known as the Art Hall and waited for him to come back. Nothing. Then the county health department said they had to dispose of the body properly, so they placed him in a tomb on the beach (urban legend says it was the same tin tub and not a tomb) and waited some more. Eventually, a hurricane hit the area, and the body vanished. Some followers at the time believed he was carried off to heaven.

"I just got a creepy feeling in the wooded area. I had only been in the area a year or so, but I love state parks." Jennifer did not know about the park's history when she went there over spring break from her teaching job. She had heard it was once the site of a cult but had never gotten the details. She just thought it was a pretty place to spend the day and get her steps in.

> *I'm walking the path and there was this little turn with some trees kind of down a little in front of me. I saw a small boy run across the path. Now, it was pretty wooded, and trees were down and there were palm fronds and leaves all over the place. He just ran across with no sound. Then he was gone. It was only ten feet in front of me, but I didn't hear him coming. I didn't see him going. It was just a flash. Then I got this sick feeling, like I had been spinning. I looked around. I put my pack down to get some water and noticed a man behind me. Not a man, but the shape of a man. He was all black, like the shadowy thing in Peter Pan. No eyes, but I could tell he was looking at me. Then he was just gone.*

The Unity movement went into decline after Teed's death. Some members formed other groups and moved away, while others just died off. Little by little, the land was sold off and the buildings taken down to save on taxes. In the early 1960s, the last person who lived on the property, Hedwig Michel, gave what was left to the state to create a new state park. She lived there until her death in 1981 and is buried on the property. Her grave is one of the places where people who go there to see ghosts get evidence. Often, they capture voices on tape, known as EVPs—sometimes

Michel speaking in German (she actually joined the group after escaping Nazi Germany).

The rangers who work the park know it to be haunted; dealing with ghosts there is all in a day's work. Many of the doors that are supposed to be locked will be found unlocked after they have been checked. Others will lock when rangers are casually trying to enter what they know should be an open door. Lights turn on and off by themselves and have to be constantly checked. Window curtains in locked buildings will be open, as if someone inside is trying to look out.

Many of the rangers avoided one spot for years. On-site, one of the buildings is now known as the bakery, but those in the know save that name for the abandoned and decrepit structure that looks out on Tamiami Trail before you enter the park. That is where the Koreshan Unity sold its bread and baked goods, which is why the sign reads, "The Koreshan Unity Inc. General Store." Over the years, it burned down and was rebuilt, and it has long been a sore spot for the people who work in the park. It is mainly used for storage now and is not safe to go into. People who enter get a bad feeling

The Koreshan Unity General Store, known by the people in the park as the Bakery.

and see dark figures dart away from them as they walk through. They hear voices while walking near the bakery and get short of breath. Many think they may be sensing the spirit of a man who committed suicide nearby on the river, perhaps trapped by the very energy Cyrus Teed was drawn to.

Nikki Marie thinks differently. After having worked in the park, she was asked to look into what might be there and get rid of what remained in the old shop. The first time she went in was during the day, with her husband. "The first floor had definite pockets of heavy energy—suppressed, stagnant energy." When they entered, they heard something shift and move at the opposite end of the room. "It was not an animal. It was like someone moving a piece of heavy furniture from one side of the living room to the other."

Molly has never been in the park. She has heard from her friends that it is haunted and has no desire to go in. "We broke down right in front of that weird building in the front of Koreshan. It was daytime, and it was still giving me the creeps." From her perspective, when people talk about it, they make it sound evil.

> *I waited for AAA there for over an hour. Me and my boyfriend tried to joke around, but the car wouldn't start, and it was too hot inside. We had to get out—right there, in front of that haunted house. I kept hearing a whistling from it. Not from the woods around it, but from it. Like someone was right inside watching us, whistling to get our attention. Then it became louder and clearer, like the person was outside and coming toward us. I saw this weird warble of air. I don't know how else to describe it: like something was there but not there, messing with the light. We spent the rest of the time in the hot car.*

That was before Nikki decided she could cleanse whatever was there. She was not a newcomer to clearing areas of energy by then, but the bakery took almost two hours—a long time, in her experience. In describing it, she keeps going back to the same word. "The energies there were stagnant for so long that I needed to put a little more elbow grease into it." The real work began when she made her way to the second floor. Six steps up, she was hit by a feeling like a wall of bricks in her chest. The air became thicker, and she could feel the energy shift. While she has never been able to confirm this, she felt the whole building may have served some time as a hospital and that some of the patients may have been suffering from illnesses like dementia or Alzheimer's. There was a little hallway to the left of the stairs leading to a pair of double doors that opened onto the road and six or seven small rooms.

The second I turned the corner, three faces popped out, all out of different rooms. They looked out and then pulled themselves back into the room. It was like they were asking, "Why are you here?" They could see and feel and hear us coming up there. I think no one had been up there in a long time.

As she was taught, Nikki clears everything counterclockwise, moving that way through each room and through the space "like an energy bulldozer," and as she moves, the spirits depart through the door she just entered. She shifts all the energy that does not need to be there anymore, understanding that those left behind often stay because they are still attached to the physical aspects of life they were drawn to when they lived. At the bakery, she felt energy and experiences on top of energy and experiences. She feels most spirits leave willingly, tired from reliving exhausting human emotions. Not so much in the bakery.

In the first room, she could feel the energy get gentler, but when she hit the second, she encountered the girl. She was between nine and twelve and was filled with sadness and confusion.

She told me that while she was there, she experienced severe abuse. Every sort of abuse. As I cleared the energy and she understood what I was there for, I could see her becoming lighter and lighter. A lot of that lower vibrational energy she was holding onto, she was able to let go of. However, she did not really want to leave, so she stayed—but stayed in a much lighter state. That made my heart happy.

As she cleared the rest of the rooms, Nikki could feel herself getting exhausted. Whatever was there had that same puzzlement and uncertainty to it as the girl. Eventually, the job was done, although she is still not sure she was able to get everything. Sometimes the spirits do a great job of hiding when they are still holding on.

That was not Nikki's first experience in the park. She'd been brought in to conduct some meditation sessions a few years before and always enjoyed it. At first, she held them outside. Depending on the time of year, it would either be dark when they started or dark by the time they finished. Although she had seen spirits for most of her life, she was there for the people who attended and not looking for an encounter: "I wasn't there with my spidey sense on." It was October, and the full moon was out. She was not facing the nearby building, one of the more active locations on the premises, known as the Planetary Court. This was the same building

Hedwig Michel had lived in before her death. All the lights there are on sensors. As they meditated in the moonlight, everyone facing the building but with their eyes closed, Nikki started to see some of the lights turn on and off. She looked around, making sure no animals were in the area but also taking note of any birds. Nothing. And not all the lights were going on, like they would if something solid was triggering them. It was just a random light followed by a random light.

"I always, prior to meditations, would cleanse and clear the energy of the space. I would create a circle and utilize a string of Christmas lights to outline where I had created that circle. People could choose to be inside or outside the circle." Nikki was on the outside so she could monitor and make sure they were safe from any supernatural energy or living thing looking to sneak up on them. "I heard a rush of energy. Not footsteps but like a strong wind. Not wind all around us but a *whoosh* of energy coming up that path toward the Planetary Court. My thought was, *Man, they're pissed. They are not cool with this. They do not want me to do meditations here*." The more she felt the energy, the more she came to see it was more curious than angry. It was female and maternal and mischievous but not angry or dangerous. Nikki almost took it as the entities giving her their blessing to continue her work on the property. She said many of the people involved in the meditation that night said they heard noises and felt a presence they had not experienced there before. That convinced her to pay attention to what was there.

The rocking chairs outside the Planetary Court have the habit of moving on their own when there is no wind blowing. They will start and stop, most often when there are children around. It is from this porch that people also get recordings of a bell being rung, as if students are being called back to class, and see a woman standing at Hedwig's grave. Visitors have taken pictures of partial humans in the windows and on the steps.

Eventually, Nikki's meditation group was moved inside the Art Hall. "With that came a whole different set of energies and a whole different experience in and of itself." Spotting ghosts became a regular thing. This is where Cyrus Teed was laid to wait for his return. The building had also been used for meetings and as a school and playhouse.

> *Many times before, during and after the meditations, we would hear children laughing. More times than not, during meditation, I would feel the wood in the floor give in a way. Very often, I know for certain, Cyrus was there with us. He had a very different energy.*

The chair at Koreshan known to move by itself and answer questions.

Sometimes she would see him sitting in a rocking chair in the back area of the building or walking around and in between the meditators. "He was not an active participant. He was more an observer."

That kind of presence is felt all over the park, and it's not always pleasant. Many report getting sick to their stomachs, especially near the building now known as the bakery. It has a glass wall that allows people to look in and see what life was like at the real bakery at the height of the group's popularity. Sometimes people, thought to be actors, are seen inside, looking confused, before fading away. But it is the feeling of being tired and your stomach turning that visitors experience time and time again.

"I remember feeling like I was drunk," says Maria of the two times she visited that area of the park. "The first time, I got all lightheaded and had to sit down. I was young. It was like being drugged." By the second time she visited the park, she had heard all about the Koreshan Unity and the ghost stories. She considered herself an empath and emotionally prepared herself for being there. "It didn't help. I got that feeling again looking through that window. I thought I saw someone looking back at me, just a face. Then I doubled over. It was like I needed throw up. I almost did. I left. You couldn't pay me to go back there."

There might be an explanation for that sensation. Rangers talk about a family that lived in that building, although no time frame is ever given. For reasons no one knows, the father started to slowly poison his wife and three kids. They died and were buried there with only rocks to mark their graves, which was a custom of many of the Koreshan Unity members, who believed burial was almost useless given that the dead would be resurrected. The rangers even say dogs brought onto the property to be trained in finding dead bodies found the family, confirming the story.

Many of the stories told at Koreshan State Park, even the ones that can't be backed up, make sense and gain an audience. The energy there is unmistakable, so every ghost story is believable, and each time one is told, the paranormal footprint of the places deepens. It could be that the energy is like that, too. It attracts and fuels and maybe even traps. It gives life to things that no longer have it and invites the weak to feed. Maybe Cyrus Teed did return, in a sense. We just aren't looking for him the right way.

CHAPTER 13

THE SAD STORY OF AMOS AND INGRID

Romeo and Juliet play out the plague on both their houses, but as the curtain closes, the audience is also satisfied—much more than the freshmen who are forced to read it in their English classes. The people who have stepped into the world of Verona may be unsettled or even dislike how things happen, but when the tale is over, they go on their way. No one ever asks what happens to the star-crossed lovers after. No one considers how the two might roam the church, looking to reunite in death or cursed to be without each other as they spend the decades close but far away. Amos and Ingrid, whom teens say haunt the Amish Bridge in Sarasota, cannot find a tragic or a happy ending. They cannot have an ending. Unlike their counterparts onstage, they keep coming back to the site of their death. We get our inspiration for the background of hauntings from the stories we know. The haunting is real, but the why is something familiar. The two teens are trapped because they cannot move on from their deaths, but they also travel to the bridge in hopes that someday they will be able to hold each other again.

There may be no hope of that. On nights when the moon is not hidden by the clouds, when the lilies are in bloom, the two spirits float from their sides of the water. Amos is said to come from the east, the Amish section of Sarasota known as Pinecraft. Ingrid comes from the west, the land of those people known as the English. They come to the edge of the water and stare at each other. There is a moment when possibility takes over their faces. Their mouths move, but you cannot hear what they are saying. They stretch their hands out to each other, weeping taking over words. Eventually, they fade away, no closer to reuniting and forced to repeat the dance if the moon beams brightly the next night.

Ghosts, you see, cannot cross water.

People living in that part of Sarasota have grown up hearing that story, and if it was just something passed on by word of mouth, it may have faded over time. Instead, the tale of lost love perseveres based on eyewitness accounts and unexplained lights. "I think it was started by people wanting their kids to stay away from a dangerous railroad bridge," says Mary. She has been a resident of Sarasota since she was a child and has heard several different versions of the story over the years. She even has a postcard, most likely bought at Yoders, the Amish restaurant near one of the spots where the phantoms are said to try to meet. "I guess it's not really known except around here. I live really close to it [the bridge], so all the kids know about it."

She tells a shortened version of the story:

> *Many years ago an Amish boy fell in love with a girl on the other side of Phillippi Creek. Since she was not Amish, their relationship was forbidden to continue. They were both so heartbroken that they ended their lives by jumping off a nearby railroad bridge. It is believed that their ghosts are now trapped on opposite sides of that bridge, each forever searching for the other.*

Elliot echoes Mary in what he has heard and how well known the story may be to residents:

> *I'm pretty sure that bridge postcard is referring to the old, dilapidated bridge down the tracks next to Der Dutchman restaurant. It has not been in use in decades. Amish used to use it to move celery they grew nearby. It was never used for cars or foot traffic, and there is no easy way to get to it. We used to play around there as kids. It was still in use at the time, in the 1980s.*

Like Mary, he knows parts of the story. Each generation adds their details, editing the story and mixing in their own sightings so the audience feels the passion the teller feels. The haunting even changes locations—in this case, perhaps to keep the kids safe from natural forces. The warning does not make much sense. Either way, it is hard to tell if the full version of the story has been chopped up over the years or formed by the retelling.

Amos is the teenage son of an Amish celery farmer in Pinecraft and often travels into the main part of the city to sell his product. One day, he sees a

An old cartoon showing just how long people have been spreading the legend of Amos and Ingrid. *Picture courtesy of Bill Miller.*

beautiful young woman hanging clothes on the line behind her house. He immediately falls in love, thinking this is the most beautiful woman he has ever seen. After several days of him rolling his cart extra slowly by her house, she finally takes notice and stops him so they can talk. She begins to fall for him as well. They both know their families will not like them together, so they make a habit of sneaking out of the house and meeting at the bridge that acts as the unofficial border between their two worlds. When he gets there, he whistles a song he learned as a child, and she pops out of the lilies laughing. They spend the night talking and holding hands, dreaming that the sun will never rise. As their love grows, they both talk of leaving Sarasota and the disapproving eyes of their families.

One night, Amos's father starts to get suspicious. He asks Amos to sit down and tell him what's been going on that has made him so distracted over the last couple of months. As the teen tries to convince his father that everything is just fine, Ingrid waits for him at the bridge. She gets bored and begins picking the lilies, pretending as she groups them together that they are her wedding bouquet. The best flowers are in the water close to

The bridge known to be where the cursed couple meets.

the bank, and while stretching to reach them, she loses her balance and falls into the water. Her leg is cut by the rocks, and her dress is now soaking wet and smeared with blood. She quickly strips down to her slip and decides to run home and change before Amos arrives, knowing it is only a few minutes' run back to her house. She leaves the dress behind so as to not bring any evidence of what she's been doing back to the house. As soon as Amos's father finally falls asleep, Amos is out the window and running to the bridge. When he gets there, he begins to whistle, but Ingrid does not jump out.

Amos climbs to the top of the bridge, and that is when he sees it. Among the rocks below is her favorite white dress, torn and spotted with blood—in the mouth of an alligator. He knows what has happened and is overwhelmed with sorrow and guilt. If he had not asked her to meet him, she would still be alive. How can he go on without her? He softly says her name and jumps from the bridge to his death. Ingrid arrives only a few minutes later, sees his body floating face down in the water and knows he is gone. She, too, is overcome and takes her own life by jumping.

Now Amos and Ingrid are trapped at the bridge, repeatedly coming on moon-soaked nights in an attempt to be reunited in death. He comes from his side and she from hers, but because ghosts are not allowed to cross water, each can only watch the other from across the water and hope for the curse to be broken.

Their story echoes that famous play by Shakespeare, but if it was just a story, it would not have lasted decades. Mary and Elliot confirm two aspects of the haunted legend; both remain firm that everyone in the neighborhood knew the story, and both have seen unexplained things at the bridge and know other people who have seen them. The haunting is real, even if the story is not.

There are enough holes in the story, if you look closely, that it must be believed and passed on for a reason. While it might be understandable to have two houses divided, the Amish and the people of Sarasota have never shown signs that they do not get along. The Amish began to arrive in the area in 1925, attracted to the warm weather and the good farming they saw in other northern parts of the state. They began to buy lots of land and spread the word. It is unclear how good the land actually was for growing celery, but their original crop adds to the lovers' story. In the decades that followed, more people came and settled, some for the winter and some taking up yearlong residency. The two groups, unlike many people in such situations, appear to have always gotten along. The Amish brought commerce and tourism money to the area, and the English respected their culture and encouraged the building of churches. There may have been some kind of tension involving romance between the two groups, but there wasn't any institutional dislike for each other.

Looking back on it, the adults who grew up with the story have rationalized why it was told to them. Most understand it as a warning to keep them away from the dangerous bridge. While it would take a fluke fall to die from tumbling from it, the real threat is from the alligators featured in the story. They pose a real danger, enough so that the story has traveled to another bridge in the area. Phillippi Creek runs east–west for a while and then shifts to run north–south. It creates the unofficial border between Pinecraft and the rest of Sarasota, with two bridges spanning the water. The first bridge is where the creek runs east–west and is the location of the original story. The second is where many people say they see the ghosts, right as the creek crosses over Bahia Vista Street.

An old railroad bridge that is more likely the origin of the Amos and Ingrid legend. *Picture courtesy of Troy Evers.*

Using a story as a warning to avoid the bridge makes sense. At night, anyone playing there is right in the path of a busy road. It had a reputation, especially in the 1970s and 1980s, for being a strip people raced down at night. There are also homeless camps on both side of the bridge. You do not see them from the road, but as soon as you walk down the embankment—or ride your bike, as is common with the Amish—they become clear. There is also the very real fear of alligators. Stop any local walking around or hanging out at the shops nearby, talk to the men fishing in the creek, even ask the woman who owns the property next to the water and they will all tell you the same thing. There are two alligators who make their home right there, and each is at least fifteen feet long. There is even lore about their grandaddy who died years ago; some measured him out at over twenty feet.

That may be a tall tale, but stories like this have to be based in need. Stories about Paul Bunyan aren't told in the desert. If your average teenager is told to avoid a place or else they risk seeing two ghosts trying to cross the water to be together, the first thing they are going to do is go there on the next full moon night to see two ghosts trying to cross the water to be together. As something to deter the young, a good legend with ghosts will not do the job.

It becomes a simple equation, then. Add the number of people who have seen something there. Subtract the number who would be scared to see a ghost and multiply by a backstory so well known that most people in the country can at least reference it. What you get is ghostly lore. The haunting is real—probably not the tale of star-crossed lovers people share but two souls trapped, wishing they could just walk across the water.

CHAPTER 14
FIRST STREET, FEAR STREET

I rarely, if ever, talk about myself in my books. I live in the realm of haunted folklore, recording stories that have been passed down, sometimes for generations, and that help define a community. I have been known to sneak my own experiences onto the page under another name or in a general sense. But I am not the story. I try to allow the tales to have their own lives. While I have been to almost all the places I write about and tried to experience them just as the community has talked about them, I let the legend take center stage.

This story is a bit different. Since early 2024, I have been walking in the footprints of an established haunted area and allowing groups of people to come along with me. While True Tours has been around for more than fifteen years, I can't help thinking that my presence has brought another dimension to it. It's a well-established road I walk down. The stories have been told and retold by different guides through the years, but since joining the team, I have uncovered other anecdotes, connected some of the common themes running through them and worked to tell the stories of the ghosts' lives and deaths in a way that brings some sort of order to the chaos of their ghostly legends.

I had always joked that Fort Myers (and Lee County in general) lacks a strong urban legend backbone due to its age and population. Most people living there were not born there, and those who were born there have not been living in the area for generations. It's just not that kind of place. A good ghost story needs time to grow and change as it moves down from one age to another and back again. Fort Myers does not have that kind

The old Heitman General Store, where Harvey worked and began his empire. *Picture courtesy of Shelley Simpson.*

of generational history. That is what I thought before I met Gina Taylor, who runs True Tours out of downtown Fort Myers. While perfecting her cemetery tour and walking history tour, Taylor brought the full force of her expertise as a historian and her connections to the history and business world of the city to craft her expeditions. As she did so, the community learned to trust her with its history, and when someone feels confident with you, ghost stories tend to come out.

The story of the City of Palms is really a tale of two cities. The first comes in the early days. It had a boom in the early part of the twentieth century and a crash some years after that. As Taylor began to walk through the history of the city, taking its pulse, stories began to emerge, most of them recent. It was as if the past was looking to speak to people by whispering into the ears of the present. It was that clash and the richness of the people involved that drew her into creating the tour, and as each character came to life for her, she felt more inspired to share the murmurs of their life after death. "I want to honor the dead by what I do. That's why I started the Haunted History Tour, and that's why I've kept it going."

The tour snakes through the downtown area, holding history and the paranormal next to each other and allowing people to decide for themselves what they think. There is one stretch of the tour more connected to the town's history than the others and more linked to the overall energy of the town. Go downtown on any night of the week and you can feel its energy. Walk down First Street on the weekend in season and you'll think you walked into New Orleans or Miami. The vibe is all around you, but if you pay attention, it's not just the party atmosphere of the present in the shops and restaurants or on the bricks that pave the road.

It's the kind of place Harvie Heitman would have been proud of.

THOSE BRICKS

First Street may have more than one reason to be haunted. Giants of Fort Myers history walked there and looked to put their mark on a rising star of a southern city. There might be something else at work, though. While it was officially incorporated in 1886, the current city was built on the ruins of several military bases that had been established during the Seminole and Civil Wars. Thomas Edison, Henry Ford and Harvey Firestone brought some fame to it, growing its reputation and attracting people from around the country to start visiting. Around that time, the first brick streets were laid down, and businesses started to flourish. It remained an active city through the 1950s, but then an odd thing happened. Like they did in many places throughout the state, things fell apart. Business left, and entrepreneurs began to board up their shops and leave for other developing places in Florida. Through the 1970s and 1980s, it was a city that began to look more and more like a ghost town.

Here's an example of what I mean. When George Romero, writer and director of *Night of the Living Dead*, came to Fort Myers in the early 1980s, he was impressed. It was not that the city was splendid. He loved that it looked like a zombie apocalypse had happened there. He thought he could shoot his new movie there without having to change much of the scenery. If you watch *Day of the Dead*, released in 1985, you'll see downtown Fort Myers in all its glory. The historic First National Bank, built in 1914, takes center stage as the zombie exit accompanied by alligators.

These kinds of things are cyclical. By the mid-1990s, business had returned, and life was coming back. City planners wanted to take advantage of the boom. They began work on a project called Streetscape in 2010. This called for the streets to be torn up and utilities to be moved underground.

The First National Bank, where George Romero decided Fort Myers looked like the perfect setting for a zombie movie.

Underneath the chipped and potholed asphalt lay the original bricks that had become the trademark of the town. Most reports put the number of bricks at five hundred thousand, but other estimates place it closer to one million. They were carefully unearthed, sent off to be cleaned and repaired and then laid down throughout Fort Myers, mostly on First Street and Hendry Street.

There are two common theories that echo their way through many ghost stories. When you change a place ghosts call home, they tend to speak up about it. Sometimes that change is a new family. Sometimes the spirits awaken when renovations are made. Change the environment, spark a haunting. There are countless stories of families who add an addition to an old house or break down a wall to create an open floor plan and then have to deal with paranormal activity. The balance of the place is disturbed. The energy can't flow the way it used to. The other theory is sometimes referred to as stone tape theory. Spirits are energy and can be trapped and stored in the same way energy can. People believe rocks and stones can effectively do this. Take something like a brick. It retains some of the spiritual energy of those around it and waits for the right situation to replay their experiences.

Put these theories together, and First Street becomes Fear Street.

The Franklin Shops

It starts with two bookends, the first of which is one of the most popular stores downtown. The Franklin Shops was first established in November 2010 in the shadow of Streetscape. The building itself had been there for almost one hundred years. It was built in 1937 under the direction of Walter Franklin, who moved his hardware store into the building a few years after serving as mayor of Fort Myers. He passed away in 1967, and the St. Vincent de Paul Thrift Shop took over. That business eventually went under, and the building lay unoccupied for years. While an influential man in the city, Mr. Franklin also was particular about his store. There was no second floor at the time, except for a mezzanine where he kept an office. If he was in, employees knew to be on guard. Without warning, he would come out of his office to make sure things were running smoothly. He would check to see no one was stealing. He would check to see if any of the employees were lazing about. Then he would disappear back into his office like he had never been there. People who worked there always felt his eyes were on them, even when he wasn't there.

When the owners decided to rebrand as the Franklin Shops, one woman was made manager, and she helped with the design and the recruiting of new vendors. Unlike the business models that had been in the space before, the new vision saw eclectic merchants renting out areas to sell their wares, giving it the feel of a marketplace. Walking in now is like taking a real-life tour through scores of Etsy pages. Construction crews started work on building a second floor to accommodate more people and installed a spiral staircase on the opposite end of the building.

It was during the construction that the weirdness started. The manager was working late one night with her mother in Walter Franklin's old office. From outside the door, she heard footsteps, like someone walking toward them on the second floor. They went out to check, but the store was dark and empty. It didn't make any sense. The place was closed and locked tight. They had not even opened for business yet. They went back into the office, leaving the door open. No sooner had the manager sat down than the steps began again, this time getting closer. Both the manager and her mother burst through the door, only to find themselves alone on the second floor, with no movement or noise coming from anywhere else in the store. Now the fear started to set in. They were two women alone in the building. More importantly, there was no actual floor laid down upstairs near the office. The skeleton had been built, but it was still under construction.

Things continued to happen after the opening. Employees talked among themselves about feeling they were being watched from the area where the old office was. The music would switch without anyone touching it. Customers asked them odd questions about items they had put aside moving when they turned their backs or purchases missing from their bags when they went to leave. One man talked about a disturbing experience at one of the vendor stands. It was set up to sell exotic and custom teas. He shopped through the choices and, not finding anything he liked, walked away. As soon as he did, he heard the sound of china cups being stirred with silverware. There was the clinking of metal against porcelain and then three taps, like making sure whatever was left on the spoon made its way back into the cup. He turned but saw no one behind him. He went to walk away and heard the same thing: several tinkles and then three taps. He turned around quickly, but again, no one was there. He walked back to investigate and then noticed something peculiar. The stand did not sell cups or silverware. It specialized only in tea.

Theories have come and gone for the last decade. Perhaps the energy brought into the store by all those different customers and all those different vendors is enough to produce a spirit. There is a long history of haunted or

The Franklin Shops, the anchor of haunted First Street and True Tours' Haunted History Tour.

cursed objects. Now imagine multiple people bringing potentially spooky items under one roof. There also might be a simpler reason.

One morning, an employee was setting up the shop for the day. He was behind the counter and counting the drawer when he heard the distinct *clang* of someone stepping onto the spiral staircase. He whipped his head up in time to see a man climbing the steps. He was not wholly there and dressed in old-fashioned clothing. He called out to the man that the store was not open yet but was ignored. The man continued to climb. The employee came out from behind the counter to follow him, calling out the entire time. The man was now walking onto the second floor. The employee made it to the top of the stairs and shouted out one more time. The man went to turn but vanished. There the employee was, in a locked building before the sun had fully come up, staring into the empty space where a weird man had just been standing.

It started with fright. Most people who experience the supernatural for the first time will quickly move into the next stage. He began to rationalize what had just happened, telling himself it must have been a trick of light, and after all, he had not been sleeping well lately. By the time the store opened, he had convinced himself it was just his imagination and worked his shift laughing at how he could have been so silly. When it came time to leave, he went up to the office to talk to the night manager. Maybe she had experienced something similar or could just be a listening ear for his unusual story. Instead, when he opened the door, he was confronted by the man he had seen on the stairs. His mouth dropped open, and he turned white. But it was not an actual person he was looking at. There on the wall hung a picture, and underneath it was the name of the founder of the building, Walter Franklin.

THE MURPHY-BURROUGHS HOUSE

The other bookend is the Murphy-Burroughs House on the corner of First and Fowler. Originally built in 1901 for a local rancher, the house became a solid part of the lore of Fort Myers when Nelson Burroughs purchased it in 1919. The house was given over to his daughters in 1922, and if you listen to Gina Taylor, that was when the real energy started to flow through its rooms. The two sisters, Jettie and Mona, could not have had personalities further apart. Their tension brought a certain energy to the house. Jettie was more proper and like a southern lady of the times, which often clashed with Mona, who was notorious for being a free spirit. "The more I studied her over time, the more I found out about her," says Taylor. "She was very avant-garde and ahead of her time. Not a prankster, more like 'girls just want to have fun.' She was always throwing parties. It's not like she was irresponsible. She just didn't act like a regular, proper woman." In the 1960s, Hurricane Donna hit Fort Myers hard. As part of the renovations after the storm, Mona asked that a porch be built so parties could be thrown there. She was entering her sixties at the time, and to this day, it is still known as Mona's Dancing Porch.

Most, including Taylor, feel Mona is the ghost who has been seen on occasion and felt more often. After her death in 1978, the house went to her husband, Franz Fischer, with the stipulation that he could live there until he passed. Then it was to be made into either a park or a house museum. He lived until 1983, and Taylor was hired on in 1990 as director of the new museum. Over the time she worked there, she held several different positions within the historical community and was responsible for different sites, but she held a special love for the Burroughs House. By 1994, the place had been nearly completely restored. Taylor kept much of the original furniture and household items but had to outsource things like the wallpaper. She even found shutters and sent them off to a professional to be repaired and reinstalled. Throughout all this, she got into the habit of talking to Mona and asking her about how she thought things were going. "I never thought I was talking to the dead or something. It was just something I did. Mona left that house to be used for fun. When something fabulous would happen, I would ask her what she thought."

The house began to host weddings in 1991, and when in full gear, there was often one on Friday night, two on Saturday and sometimes one or two on Sunday. It was after one of these weddings that Taylor thinks she may have caught her first glimpse of Mona. She and another woman had just worked back-to-back weddings. They were dead on their feet. At the time, Taylor was also a single mother working full time as a historian while running events for the city. "The garbage cans were overflowing, and we needed to get everything out for the guys on Monday morning. I asked Nancy if there was any chance she just wanted to come back on Sunday to clean up." Both women agreed, locked up and set the alarm system.

The parking lot out back was dark, but the ladies knew it well enough to find their way to their cars. The oak tree out there had been set up with lights during the last wedding, but they had been turned off a while ago. The attic had windows that faced the back. It was always locked with a padlock, and only those who worked there had access to the key. As they got ready to leave, they noticed the light in the attic was on.

"It was bizarre. I thought, *Who could have gotten into the attic?*" Neither woman even remembered having used the room that day. They argued over who might be up there and whether or not to go up and check.

All of a sudden, there is this woman standing in the window. I couldn't tell if she was looking down at us. She has this long veil on. It was an off-white veil, but that could have been the lighting. I couldn't see her face. To this day, all these years later, it is clear as bell.

Both refused to go in there and just took off. "I wasn't going to confront whatever was up there." When Taylor thinks back on it now, she remembers two things. The first is that she never felt truly comfortable in the attic. The second is that right around the time the woman appeared, Taylor had been going through a steam trunk in the attic and found some person items of Mona's, including an old camera with pictures left on the film. She sent the film off to be developed (a specialist was unable to retrieve anything) and brought the camera and some of the other items down to the museum for a new display. Perhaps this triggered whoever was in the window.

The other incident took place a while later. Most museum homes are closed on Mondays to be cleaned and so the people who run them can catch up on paperwork. That Monday, Gina was there with Phillip, a man originally hired as a groundskeeper who eventually helped with event setup and cleanup. Over the years, Taylor had grown to enjoy these easy Mondays where the two of them would talk and enjoy each other's company. They worked mainly in the old guest house on the grounds, separate from the main house, and would not turn the alarms off. One morning, Phillip could not find a broom he used to sweep the outside steps in a storage area not connected to the house. They both assumed someone had borrowed it during the wedding and misplaced it in the kitchen. Phillip turned the alarm off and entered the house.

As he searched for the broom, he heard what he thought was running water coming from the second floor. Inside the bathroom, the water was running, and the old-fashioned tub, a remnant from the original house, was almost full.

He turns it off and comes running into my office. He told me the bathtub was almost full. I said, "What are you talking about?" He wasn't thinking logic. He was spooked, and he got me spooked. He was the one who turned the motion detectors off, so he knew if anyone had been in there, he would have seen them. He knew something was going on.

The water was turned off in time to stop a flood that would have damaged the newly painted living room right below.

The same thing happened two more times, both on Mondays. They brought a plumber out to check and see if there was a reason the water would turn on by itself, but after a careful examination, he said everything was normal. The third time, when Phillip entered the house, all the taps in the bathroom were open, as well as the kitchen. Taylor knows what she thinks explains it.

> *Did she only take baths on a Monday when no one was there? She had privacy. Did I take her privacy away. I was kidding all the time with her. Now, looking back on this and knowing more about the paranormal, maybe there was something happening there, like an exchange of energy. I stood on that big, beautiful staircase and said, "Mona, cut it out. I know it's you."*

It never happened again after that.

HARVIE AND THE BRADFORD

In the middle of these two buildings is the heart of downtown, and if he were alive today, Harvie Heitman would approve of what the city has become.

If you approach First Street from Jackson, you see two buildings in front of you. On the right is the Sidney and Berne Davis Art Center (SBDAC), the cultural center of Fort Myers. On the left is the Blue Boutique, perhaps the nicest Goodwill in the country.

The property that houses the Sidney and Berne Davis Art Center has a long history. It is said there was a Calusa settlement right on that spot before parts of the original fort were built there. That burned, and eventually, a library stood on the spot before that was condemned and razed. Manuel Gonzalez, Fort Myers's first settler, chose that spot to build his house. In 1933, the current building was erected and made into a post office. Later, the post office was turned into a federal courthouse, which eventually moved across town into a more modern facility in 1998. Fort Myers took over control of the building and leased it to Florida Arts for a dollar per year for a term of ninety-nine years, allowing the art center to be born.

As part of the renovations, Gina Taylor was brought in for expertise on Fort Myers's history and the building itself. She was often in it with only the work crews. The air-conditioning had been turned off, historical aspects of the interior had been ignored or covered up and mold had been allowed to grow. There was work to be done. One day, Gina was touring the second floor of the building while the crews worked downstairs. She came to the corner room and noticed the window was open. She climbed over all the construction and closed it, wondering who would have left it open. She and the work crews were the only ones allowed in the building. They all left a little while later, but when Gina got outside, she noticed the window was open again. That was impossible. She went back into the building to close it again, but by the time she reached the street for the second time, unseen hands had, again, opened it. During the entire renovation, the window would not stay closed. This does not happen anymore, though. It might be that the renovations are complete, but more likely, it's due to those who ran the building becoming so annoyed that they sealed it so it could never be opened.

Before it was ever a post office or a courthouse or an art center, the private residence of Harvie Heitman stood on the property. His family ran their business, the Heitman General Store, across the street, where the Blue Boutique Goodwill is now. He had the easiest commute in the world. His vision was to see Fort Myers be the jewel of the state and compete with cities like Tampa and Miami, and from that store, he set about growing his empire. He expanded the building to stretch down the street, establishing the Bradford Hotel in 1905. The hotel was also financed by Tootie and Ambrose McGregor, who asked that it be named after their son, who had died. Instead of the continental breakfast many establishments offered, Harvie gave guests the "American Deal," serving all three meals. His model included establishing businesses on the first floor. The businesses would be fueled by the hotel and draw more customers to it.

Harvie passed away in 1922. After a fight between his wife and brother, she exhumed his body and moved it back to her hometown in New Jersey, although his plot remains in the Fort Myers Cemetery. Eventually the business changed hands, and the Bradford Hotel was closed. It was broken up and turned into the Bradford Apartments, and the vibe of the place changed.

After the conversion, people living in the rooms started to see a man walking the halls. They all described him the same way. He is wearing fancy, old-fashioned clothes, and on his head sits a top hat. The second and third floors of the building are a bit of a maze. One hallway leads you all the way through, but that hall snakes, turning this way and that, with mirrors on most of the walls. Residents see the man with the top hat in the mirror, but when they take one of the angled turns, he is no longer there.

The elevator inside the Bradford Apartments where the Man in the Top Hat is seen.

He is never seen in the apartments themselves, but take a turn here and a turn there and there's a chance you'll catch a glimpse of him rounding the corner. Some have even taken the elevator on the second floor and seen him approach. They hit the button to open the door, not thinking anything is unusual, but when the door opens a second later, he is gone. There have even been a few reports of him stepping into the elevator, but then the door opens and no one is in it.

A woman who lives in the apartments took the tour with me one Halloween. She allowed us up there, and it took walking those halls for me to understand what the witnesses were talking about. The woman said she has never seen him, but others talk about seeing a man in a top hat who disappears in the hall. She did say that her father was part of team who converted the hotel. The workers were allowed to take things from the site that were not going to be used. Several were given to her as she was setting up her apartment. The one gift she refused was one of the mirrors from the hallway. She said she got a creepy feeling from it that she could not explain and politely refused it.

In 2019, a woman named Michelle took a new job as director of the Fort Myers Redevelopment Agency, with offices around the block from where the Heitman General Store once stood. From her first day, she did not feel right about the office. There was a dark, uninviting feel to it. She invited her friend who was a psychic to check things out and maybe cleanse the place. When her friend didn't show up at the time they agreed, Michelle called her. Her friend told her to come outside, where she saw her staring at the monuments outside the Sidney and Berne Davis Art Center. Without turning, Michelle's friend asked her, "Who is the guy in the hat?" She claimed she saw a man appear out of nowhere; walk across the street, ignoring the traffic; and then approach the Goodwill and disappear. When Michelle later told the story to Gina Taylor, things clicked. That was the path that Harvie took.

There are many things that may create a ghost. That walking across the street to work sounds much like what they call a psychic recording, or a loop of an activity a ghost did while it was alive. Harvie's ghost is more complex than that. He is also a spirit disturbed. His body has been removed from its grave and taken away from the city he loved. But there is even more to it. Fort Myers is now the city he envisioned. All his hard work and dreaming have come to pass, and maybe he feels the need to check up on it and even bask in atmosphere of the city he helped create.

THE SHOPS

Harvie doesn't just stay in the apartments. The businesses underneath the Bradford suffer their own versions of a haunted house. The Naples Soap Company is known for having some of the best product in the downtown area. The employees, however, never know when their day is going to start with having to reshelve. Some days, they come in and find all the soap tossed on the floor and the glass candles placed in strange spots by a mischievous hand. This will happen for a few days in a row until the manager—and it has to be the manager—tells them to stop. The manager's authority is enough to pause the activity for a few months. Then the store is a mess again.

Belgian Yummies was a staple of First Street until it recently closed at that location. It seems to have moved to another address in Fort Myers, which may be for the better. On the Haunted History Tour, people would get pictures of an odd fog in the restaurant while taking shots of another haunted building next door. They'd ask if there were any stories about the restaurant. I always had to shrug my shoulders and tell them that I had not heard anything about it myself, but perhaps it was the same man who walked the Bradford with a hat. A few pictures even seemed to show the reflection of someone wearing something on his head. That was until I got to the end of the tour one night and a man took me aside. He was from Belgium and was in town on business. He told me he had just bought the ice cream shop. I laughed, saying I was surprised he still wanted it after the stories he had just heard about First Street, and he put his hand on my shoulder and leaned in close. "It makes sense now. I got it for a steal. The owner said he didn't want to have to deal with the unexplained fires that kept happening there. Whatever happened to him in that building, he just wanted out."

I added his words to the tour and made more of an effort to focus on Belgian Yummies. A few weeks later, I noticed a pair of Florida Gulf Coast University students on a tour looking in and jokingly pushing each other. They kept giggling. I asked them what was so funny. One told me her father was a Fort Myers firefighter. Everyone on the force knew about the shop. The fires there were the stuff of urban legend because not one of the fireman could explain how the fires started or why they seemed to happen only there. New firemen were often the ones forced to go out and investigate, as a way to initiate them. According to one of the girls, they even have a file on all the fires and mishaps there, held in the same regard as folder full of Skunk Ape sightings.

I was once approached by an employee from Arts for Act as I waited outside for the tour to begin. I knew that there was once a time when we talked about the studio on the tour. The main story involved a ghost cat customers reported in the back, although no one who worked there had a cat or ever actually saw one themselves. The employee was waiting to load boxes into a car and noticed my headset and True Tours badge.

"Do you do the tour?" she asked, looking back at the studio to see if anyone was watching.

She then told me about a problem that the studio had been having lately. Employees listen to the radio sometimes during the day, and a voice kept coming over the speakers. She told me it was loud enough to tell someone was talking but not at a volume where they could understand what was being said. At first, they thought it was an issue with the speakers and changed them out. The conversations continued. It just became part of the allure of the store, and they stopped trying to explain it. On First Street, business owners just get used to the weirdness. Then one day, an employee decided to catch them in the act. She quickly turned the volume all the way down. She heard an audible "Shush," although she was alone in the store. Apparently, the ghosts wanted to warn each other to not be heard.

THE ARCADE THEATRE

Originally built by Harvie in 1915 underneath the Bradford, the Arcade Theatre is now the home of the Florida Repertory Theatre. If you approach it from Bay Street, the building is bright and inviting. You can often see people taking their picture next to it when there is no show going on. It is a bit different from First Street, which you can only find by going through a series of doors. It's a small but successful company, bringing in popular shows that draw people into the downtown.

It also has its share of ghosts. It is sometimes said that a theater cannot be a real theater unless it has a ghost. Maybe it's the deep superstitions of the theater community or the energy brought in by the audience and the creative people who make the show go on. There are many traditions in that world, including one the Arcade participates in. Every night, they leave a single light burning on the stage. This is known as a ghost light and is supposed to keep the theater safe and the spirits away. It does not do its job on Fear Street.

When Kim Cool was writing her book *Haunted Theatres of Southwest Florida*, she recorded some of the stories of ghosts people tell there. One is believed to be an actor and acting teacher named Niels Miller who died in 2007. His ghost touches people in the audience and is seen walking the theater during performances. Another is a caretaker who is seen so often that people no longer feel alarmed by his presence. He is dressed like a janitor and is usually seen in the balcony, an area used mainly for storage these days. One day, before a performance, some people spotted him up there, but he was waving his arms and frantically pointing up at the lights above the stage. They looked at him and then at the lights, but when they focused again on the balcony, he was gone. It was unsettling enough that they checked the lighting before the show. Some of the rigging was loose and might have fallen onto the actors during the performance. They tightened it up and thanked their guardian angel.

The Arcade Theatre, home to several ghostly legends.

Gina Taylor heard a few different stories when she talked to people. One involved an odd man who attended a show. A couple took their seats and noticed a disheveled man sitting a few rows ahead of them. The smell coming off him was horrendous, like he had walked out of the grave. They noticed that their friends on the other end of the theater were just sitting down in the same row as the man. During the play, the odor was unbearable and getting worse. They went outside during intermission just to get some fresh air. They asked their friends, who also came out, how they could stand to be even closer to the man. "What man?" they responded. They were alone in their row. When they all went back in for the second act, the man was gone.

There is also a story about a couple of the set designers who stayed late to paint and work on the sets for the next show. The Arcade was locked up tight, and it was just the two of them. They did not hear a sound as they worked, but when they looked up, they saw a man standing near the doors. At first, they thought it was an actor because he was wearing fancy clothes and on his head was a top hat. They called out to him that the theater was closed and he could not be there. He ignored them. They got more nervous and more scared as he walked closer to the stage, ignoring their calls as if they were not there. He then took two steps onto the stage and disappeared in front of them.

And a Final Little Glitch

And then there is this story, which in many ways is a perfect example of the shadowy and elusive nature of the ghosts of First Street.

I had finished my tour and walked back to my car shortly after ten o'clock that night. Through a friend of a friend, I am able to park at a business behind the Gwynne Institute, which is haunted by the ghost of the old miser of a principal and maybe a trapped student or two. I make jokes during the tour, while participants are trying to capture one of the ghosts peeking through the windows, that they all get to go home, but I have to go back to the building to get my car. It gets a good laugh, but to be honest, I am not scared when I return. I am usually too excited after a good tour. I do always notice that my phone tends to not have service in the parking lot. I shrug it off and wait until I am on Hendry Street before I even attempt to click on my Audible app.

This night was no different. I pulled out of my spot and began making my way to First Street. At the time, I was relistening to *The Lovely Bones* by Alice Sebold. If you are unfamiliar with the novel or the movie Peter Jackson made based on it, it's about a teenage girl who is assaulted and murdered by her neighbor. The book is told from her perspective as a ghost observing her family dealing with the grief of her death and the attempts to catch the

The stairs that the ghost of Walter Franklin climbs.

man who killed her (the movie focuses much more on the latter, while it is only a subplot of the book). At some point, her father becomes convinced he knows who the guilty man is and is determined to catch him. He becomes obsessed, and at one point, he begins to just repeat the man's name in his mind, over and over.

My car was mostly silent except for the humming of the air conditioner and a few strains of music coming in from my open window as I passed some of the bars and clubs that line the streets. I pulled up to the stop sign, notoriously one of the busiest intersections on First Street, with the Sidney and Berne Davis Art Center and Harvie's old home to my right and the Goodwill that used to be Heitman's General Store to my left. Just then, Sebold's voice came over my radio, chanting the name of the killer.

"Harvey, Harvey, Harvey, Harvey."

The odd thing is, I listened to that section of the book earlier in the day. The part where the father chants the name of his daughter's killer, George Harvey, had passed more than ten minutes ago in Audible time.

It's the kind of moment that happens all the time amid the hustle of Fear Street.

BIBLIOGRAPHY

Alexander, Eve. *Ghost Stories of Punta Gorda: An Anthology of 20 Spooky Stories.* Self-published, 2019.

———. "Who Killed Marshall Bowman?" Southwest Florida Walking Tours, January 2019. https://southwestfloridawalkingtours.com/who-killed-marshall-bowman-suspect-1-isaiah-cooper.

———. "Why Was McGraw's Place Known as the Bucket of Blood?" Southwest Florida Walking Tours. January 2019. https://southwestfloridawalkingtours.com.

Black, Joyce Turner. "Fort Myers Yesterdays." *News-Press* (Fort Myers, FL), September 15, 1963.

Burge, Laura Hildick. *Singing River Story*. Apeli, 2005.

Canfield, Nicole. "Is Fort DeSoto Park in Florida Haunted." Exemplore.com, January 14, 2014. http://exemplore.com.

Carlson, Charles. *Weird Florida*. Sterling, 2005.

Colcord, Ester B. *True Tales of Adventure and Mystery in Lee County, Florida.* Prudy's Press, 1991

Cool, Kim. *Haunted Theatres of Southwest Florida*. Historic Venice Press, 2009.

Country Living, Country Skills. "The Legend of Bloody Bucket Road." October 13, 2003. http://www.kountrylife.com.

Dr. Seuss. *What Was I Scared Of?* Random House, 1961.

Folklore of Florida (blog). "The Ghost Bridge in Pinecraft Amish Village." January 2024. https://floridafolk.blogspot.com/2016/12/the-ghost-bridge-of-amish-village.html.

Genesis, Rebecca. "Haunted History of Fort DeSoto Park." Ghostseekers.com, May 18, 2017. http://ghostseers.com.

Govoni, Jane, Mary Spoto and Valerie Wright. *Lions, Leos, and Learners: A History of Saint Leo University*. Kendall Hunt, 2013.

Hoes, David. "Bizarre Arcadia." Phantoms and Monsters, October 11, 2012. https://www.phantomsandmonsters.com.

Jenkins, Greg. *Florida's Ghostly Legends and Haunted Folklore: South and Central Florida*. Pineapple, 2013.

Lisk, Nettie. "Legends of Silver Springs." *Ocala (FL) Evening Star*, June 12, 1907.

Mahlor, Carol. "Happy 130th Birthday Arcadia." DeSoto County Historical Society, May 17, 2024. https://www.historicdesoto.org.

McCarthy, John F. "A History of the Myakka River, Sarasota County, Florida." Document prepared by the Sarasota County Historical Archives Staff, January 1, 1983.

Miller, William D. *Tampa Triangle Dead Zone*. Tampa Triangle Books, 1987.

News-Press (Fort Myers, FL). "More Views Given Anent Skeletons." September 25, 1913.

Pray, Rusty. "Cemetery's Spirits Lie in Its Stories." *Punta Gorda (FL) Sun*, October 26, 2018.

Rebman, Kimberly P. *Haunted Florida: A Guide to the Departed Soul, Volume One*. Self-published, 2008.

Rife, Susan L. "A History of 'Plain People.'" *Herald Tribune* (Tampa, FL), May 21, 2006.

Russell, Nan. "Ghosts Won't Cross Water and the Walls Speak." https://mymanatee.contentdm.oclc.org/digital/collection/p16681coll2/id/6611.

Sarasota (FL) Herald-Tribune. "The Manatee River's Legend." January 2004.

Shortuse, Marcy. "Haunted Arcadia." *Gasparilla Island Magazine* (September 2016).

St. Petersburg (FL) Times. "Anclote, in Existence 385 Years, Figures in Legends." November 7, 1932.

Stark, Brandy. "Ft. Desoto." Urban Legends of Pinellas County, May 7, 2018. http://urbanlegendsofflorida.homestead.com.

Tiffani. "Cindy: The Wandering Ghost of Anclote Road." Haunted727, January 4, 2024. https://haunted727.tumblr.com/post/77612419008/cindy-the-wandering-ghost-of-anclote-road.

Warner, Joe G. *The Singing River: A History of the People, Places, and Events Along the Manatee River*. Manatee Historical Society, 1992.

Warren, Michael. "Koreshan State Historic Site: 'The Ghosts of Florida's New Jerusalem.'" FloridaTraveler.com, March 7, 2024. https://floridatraveler.com/koreshan-state-park.

About the Author

Christopher Balzano is a writer, researcher, folklorist and current host of the podcast *Tripping on Legends*. He has been documenting the unexplained since 1994 and has been a figure in the paranormal world through his book, articles and work as the director of Massachusetts Paranormal Crossroads and, now, *Tripping on Legends*.

Balzano is the author of several books about regional hauntings, including *Dark Woods: Cults, Crime and the Paranormal in the Freetown State Forest* and *Ghosts of the Bridgewater Triangle*, as well as the collection of true ghost stories *Ghostly Adventures and Haunted Objects: Stories of Ghosts on Your Shelf* and the how-to paranormal books *Picture Yourself Ghost Hunting* and *Picture Yourself Capturing Ghosts on Film*.

He has been a contributor to Jeff Belanger's *Encyclopedia of Haunted Places* and *Weird Massachusetts* and was one of the writers behind *Weird Hauntings*. He has appeared in more than two dozen other books, often called in to offer insight into the paranormal or perspective on a certain case.

He has published three titles about haunting in Florida for Arcadia/The History Press: *Haunted Florida Love Stories*, *Haunted Ocala National Forest* and *The Ghostly Tales of Ocala National Forest*.

He has appeared on radio stations across the country and throughout the Internet, as well as being called on by television shows to comment on ghosts and urban legends, including the British television series *Conversations with a Serial Killer*. He has been a guest on *Coast to Coast AM* and been asked in as a consultant on televisions shows like *Paranormal State* and *Ghost Adventures*. He formerly ran the Paranormal News at Ghostvillage and headed up Ghostvillage for Kids.